WALKING IN
THE CITY OF THE DEAD
A Visitor's Guide

Also by Jeffrey A. Nedoroscik

THE CITY OF THE DEAD:
A History of Cairo's Cemetery Communities

Order this book online at www.trafford.com
or email orders@trafford.com

Most Trafford titles are also available at major online book retailers.

Printed in the United States of America.

ISBN: 9781426936852 (sc)
ISBN: 9781426937330 (e)

*Our mission is to efficiently provide the world's finest, most comprehensive book publishing
service, enabling every author to experience success. To find out how to publish your book,
your way, and have it available worldwide, visit us online at www.trafford.com*

Trafford rev. 8/09/2010

 www.trafford.com

North America & international
toll-free: 1 888 232 4444 (USA & Canada)
phone: 250 383 6864 ♦ fax: 812 355 4082

for Paige, Patrick & Ryan

LIST OF ILLUSTRATIONS
AND PHOTOGRAPHS

CONTENTS

ACKNOWLEDGEMENTS

I would like to thank the people of the City of the Dead for making me feel at ease wandering among the various tombs and monuments of the cemeteries that are discussed in this book. In addition, I would like to thank the many people who encouraged me to write this book -- a guide for those who wish to explore a part of Islamic Cairo that is off the beaten track. Also, I would like to thank El Sayed (Essam) Mohamed for accompanying me to the cemeteries on numerous occasions to assist me when my Arabic language abilities were unsuccessful as well as Mamdoah Abbass for originally introducing me to the City of the Dead. Without our chance meeting in Midan Tahrir, I most likely would have never become intimate with – not only the incredible monuments of the City of the Dead – but with its people as well -- something that would lead me on a new journey and change the course of my life.

PREFACE

I first became interested in the City of the Dead in 1990 as a study abroad student at the American University in Cairo. By chance, I befriended a man who lived in the Southern Cemetery of the City of the Dead. It was there that I was introduced to a society of poor but proud individuals and families. It was also there that I found some of the most remarkable tombs and monuments that the Islamic world has to offer. I wanted to know more about this unique cemetery community.

I left Egypt when my study abroad semester finished only to return again in 1992. This time, I came to Egypt as a Thomas J. Watson research fellow. My research project was called "Homelessness in Cairo's City of the Dead" and I spent one year exploring the cemeteries of the City of the Dead. Whereas my project mainly focused on the lives of the people who had made the tombs of the cemeteries their informal housing, I also spent a lot of time exploring the historical, architectural and religious importance of the tombs and mausoleums of the cemeteries. These monuments represent the history of Islam in Egypt and are a testimony to Cairo's evolution as an Islamic city.

The notes of my time in the City of the Dead grew into a manuscript of the cemeteries' history and my personal experiences with the people who live among the tombs. This book, The City of the Dead: A History of Cairo's Cemetery Communities (Bergin & Garvey, 1997) focuses primarily on the use of the cemeteries as informal housing for Cairo's urban poor and is aimed at an audience of students and scholars of Middle Eastern studies, development studies, and anthropology/sociology.

I soon became aware, however, that the City of the Dead is a curiosity for many types of people outside of the academic world and that there was a void of information on the cemeteries for the general public. What was needed was a practical guide to the City of the Dead complete with maps and walking tours for the adventurous who seek to explore this labyrinth of tombs, mosques, and mausoleums. The lack of such a guide and the encouragement of friends and colleagues prompted me to write this book. I hope that this guide becomes a useful tool for those who want to explore the wonders of the cemeteries on foot or simply from the comfort of their living room sofa.

J. Nedoroscik
Washington DC
2010

"Whatever parallels the reader may attempt to construct in order to visualize this unique zone [the City of the Dead] will be incorrect. Neither the image of a European-American cemetery (or even one in Turkey or the Fertile Crescent) nor of a bidonville will set one on the right track. There is literally no precedent – at least for its inhabitants and their problems. It is perhaps best, then, to empty one's mind totally and take a tour through the streets and perhaps a detour into history."

Janet L. Abu Lughod
<u>Cairo: 1001 Years the City Victorious</u>

CHAPTER 1
Introduction

- *What is the City of the Dead?*
- *The City of the Dead throughout History*
- *The Modern City of the Dead*
- *Islamic Art and Architecture*
- *Tips for Visitors*
- *How to Use This Guide*

WHAT IS THE CITY OF THE DEAD?

The City of the Dead has been the main burial ground for Egypt's capital city since the Arab invasion of Egypt in A.D. 640. Over the last thirteen centuries, the area that began as a few scattered tombs in the desert has grown to encompass more than five square miles of land and has earned its place in the heart of Cairo and in the annals of Egypt's Islamic history.

The City of the Dead is a group of vast cemeteries that lie to the east of contemporary Cairo's downtown area. The modern Salah Salem Highway severs the City of the Dead into various parts that were once organically joined. There are five main cemeteries: the Cemetery of the Great; the Southern Cemetery; the Northern Cemetery; the Bab al-Nasr Cemetery; and the Bab al-Wazir Cemetery.

The City of the Dead

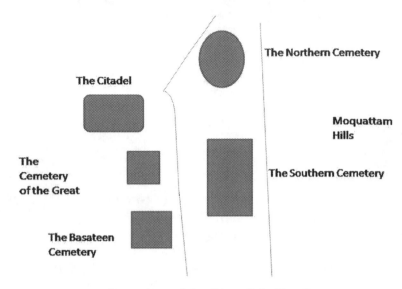

The Citadel

The Northern Cemetery

Moquattam
Hills

The
Cemetery
of the Great

The Southern Cemetery

The Basateen
Cemetery

Overview of the City of the Dead

The Cemetery of the Great is south of the Citadel (the great fortress overlooking old Cairo built between A.D. 1176 – 1193 by Salah al-Din) and is largely on the west side of Salah Salem Highway. It runs alongside the ancient aqueduct that once brought water from the Nile to the Citadel.

The Southern Cemetery is on the opposite side of the highway from the Cemetery of the Great and extends from the eastern entrance of the Citadel out to the borders of the modern Cairo suburb of Maadi. The southern tip of this cemetery is more contemporary and is typically referred to as the Basateen Cemetery. The steep slopes of the Moquattam Hills flank the Southern Cemetery's eastern side.

The Northern Cemetery begins at the north-east corner of the Citadel complex and extends northward to the boundaries of Nasr City, another of Cairo's modern suburbs. It is situated between two highways: Salah Salem Highway on the west and the Autostrade Highway on the east.

Located across Salah Salem Highway from the Northern Cemetery is the Bab al Nasr Cemetery. This burial ground extends from the ancient Fatimid (Shi'ite Muslims from North Africa who ruled Egypt from 969 - 1171) gate of the same name out towards the heart of the section of Cairo called Abbassia.

Finally, wrapping around the north-west corner of the Citadel complex is the Bab al-Wazir Cemetery.

Together, these cemeteries form what is popularly called the City of the Dead. Four of these cemeteries - those with the most important and accessible monuments - are covered in this book.

Stretching across a significant portion of Cairo's[1] physical space, the City of the Dead is a tapestry of square and rectangular interlocked buildings with the occasional mosque, monastery or shrine breaking the monotony of newer structures. The tombs that form this cemetery city typically consist of a permanent structure of one or more rooms along with a *howsh* (a walled courtyard). The quality of the materials used to build the tombs as well as the size of the tombs can vary significantly and depend on the wealth and status of the family the tomb was built for. Some of the tombs have spacious rooms covered with roofs and are furnished to accommodate the family of the deceased during visits to the cemetery. Other tombs are no more than four simple brick walls.

---

1   This reference to Cairo is referring to the municipal boundaries of Cairo which exclude Giza, as Giza is its own municipality.

The Northern Cemetery

The bodies of the deceased of the family are normally interred in underground tombs built beneath the rooms or courtyards. A single opening typically leads into the underground cavity where the remains of the males and the females are kept separate. Stone slabs cover the opening and the stairs leading into the chamber. These slabs are then covered with a thin layer of dirt. The dirt and stones are removed in the event of the passing away of a family member and a typical Egyptian Muslim burial is carried out.

In Egypt, Muslims adopted many of the burial practices that existed in pre-Islamic times. First, the rites of ablution (the washing of the body) are performed as passages from the Qur'an[2] are read out loud. Then, the body is dried and pieces of cloth are stitched around it, secured at the head and feet. The body is placed on a bier, covered with a shawl, and brought to the family tomb where the grave has been opened in preparation for the burial. The body is placed in

2   In this manuscript, I am using the spelling of 'Qur'an' to describe the Muslim holy book. The spelling 'Koran' is also widely used in English.

4

the tomb, the head is turned to face the holy city of Mecca, Saudi Arabia and the body has found its eternal earthly home. The burial completed, the tomb is then sealed once again.

Among the traditional tombs, Islamic monuments such as mosques and monasteries are scattered throughout the City of the Dead. These monuments represent every stage of Islamic history in Egypt. These mosques, monasteries, shrines, schools, and mausoleums demonstrate the diverse architectural styles and artistic techniques and trends of Islam over the centuries. Many of these monuments are well-preserved and bear witness to the political and religious leaders that held power in Egypt and who established Cairo as a great Islamic city.

THE CITY OF THE DEAD
THROUGHOUT HISTORY

The oldest part of the City of the Dead is the Cemetery of the Great. This area became a Muslim burial ground soon after Amr Ibn al-As' army[3] conquered Egypt and subdued the local, mostly Coptic Christian (Egyptian Christian), population. The earliest tombs of this cemetery pre-date the founding of the city of Cairo (A.D. 971). Rather, they were the burial grounds of al-Fustat, the capital of Egypt before the invasion by the Fatimids, Shi'ite Muslims[4] from North Africa.

Whereas al-Fustat was eventually destroyed and replaced by Cairo as Egypt's seat of power, the Islamic tombs of the cemetery were left intact and the burial ground continued to be used and expanded by each successive regime that gained control of Egypt's government. In her classic history of Cairo, Cairo: 1001 Years the City Victorious, Janet Abu Lughod writes,

---

3 Amr ibn al-As Arab armies conquered Egypt, then a province of the Byzantine Empire, in A.D. 639.

4 A Shiite is a member of a sect of Islam that believes that Ali, a cousin of the prophet Muhammad, was his first true successor. The Shiites are doctrinally opposed to the Sunni Muslims.

The extension of this cemetery [the Cemetery of the Great] northward paralleled the extension of the city of Fustat, but it is significant that while the city of the living of Fustat has long disappeared, its cities of the dead – much expanded – continue to house thousands of residents of the contemporary city.

> In A.D. 969, the Fatimid Caliph al-Muizz li-Din Allah sent an army of 100,000 soldiers under the command of General Gawhar al-Siqilly into Egypt. This army easily conquered al-Fustat and created an Egyptian Caliphate that would last for over 200 years in Egypt.

The invasion by the Fatimids brought a major change to Egypt by ushering in a period of minority (Shi'ite) rule over the majority (Sunni). Egyptians were primarily Sunni Muslims whereas their new rulers were of the Shi'ite sect of Islam. The Sunni Muslims believe that the sunna, a collection of the traditions of the Prophet and interpretations of Qur'anic law (literally 'a path'), is as powerful as the Qur'an itself. Upon the Prophet Muhammad's death, there was no clear successor. Sunni Muslims decided that a Caliph (a caliph is a successor to the Prophet Muhammad) would be elected to power. Shi'ite Muslims, however, believe that the Qur'an is absolute and divine and that the line of power should only continue through Muhammad's family. The Fatimids were named after the Prophet Muhammad's youngest daughter and believed that 'Ali, a cousin of the Prophet, was the rightful heir to power.

Not wanting to base its rule out of a city with its traditions already established, the Fatimids soon began construction on their own capital city not far away from al-Fustat. This new walled city was named al-Qahira ("the Victorious") and would become known across the world as Cairo. It became Egypt's capital city in A.D. 973.

The Fatimids intended al-Qahira to be a private, fortified enclosure. The new city housed some 20,000 – 30,000 people including the Fatimid Caliph, members of the Fatimid government, Fatimid soldiers, and servants of the Fatimids. The Egyptian middle class continued to reside in al-Fustat, separated from al-Qahira by a large swamp. No ordinary citizen was allowed to enter al-Qahira unless he or she was needed for some purpose by the Fatimids. Still, the populations of both cities continued to use the early burial grounds of the Cemetery of the Great as their main cemetery, expanding the graveyard northward towards the walls of al-Qahira. There are numerous surviving tombs from this period that illustrate the typical Fatimid style of funerary architecture.

Even during the early stages of its growth, the City of the Dead was not only used as a burial ground but was also an active part of the community -- a concept that is difficult for most westerners to comprehend. From the beginning of its formation, tomb-keepers and their dependents set up residence within the cemeteries' borders, schools and monasteries were built among the tombs, the poor and sick sought refuge in the cemeteries and criminals hid from the law among the tombs.

In A.D. 1065, a seven year famine ravished Egypt and caused a political crisis for the Fatimids -- a catastrophe that they would not overcome. By the middle of the twelfth century, the Fatimid Empire was in its final days of power.

Salah al-Din Yusuf al-Ayyubi (also popularly written as 'Saladin' in the West), a Kurd[5] from Syria, helped to bring the Fatimid Dynasty to defeat. In A.D. 1169, Salah al-Din became Prime Minister of Fatimid Egypt. Salah-al-Din was a Sunni Muslim and he did not share the religious beliefs of the more conservative Shi'ite Fatimids. Given this, he set out to return Egypt to the Sunni fold of Islam.

By A.D. 1175, Salah al-Din had wrestled power from the Fatimids and the Abbassid[6] Caliphate in Baghdad declared him Ruler of Egypt, North Africa, Nubia[7], Western Arabia, and Syria. Salah al-

---

5   A Kurd is a native or inhabitant of a mountainous region of western Asia.

6   The Abbasids were an Arabic Dynasty that expanded the Muslim empire and was named for al-Abbass, the paternal uncle of the Prophet Muhammad.

7   Nubia is an ancient region of northeastern Africa along the Nile River made up of southern Egypt and northern Sudan. Much of what was Nubia is under modern-day Lake Nasser.

Din did not claim legitimacy to rule based on lineage. Rather, he based it on the upholding of Sunni beliefs. Salah al-Din wanted to re-educate Egyptians in the Sunni faith. As a result, he sought to abolish all traces of Shi'ism in Egypt and destroyed many Fatimid monuments. He was unable to destroy the Fatimid tombs in the Cemetery of the Great, however, as this would have been a grave sin. The saints entombed in these Fatimid shrines are revered by both Sunni and Shi'ites alike.

Under Salah al-Din's leadership, Egypt once again became the center of the Muslim world as his dynasty solidified its power in the region. Unlike the Fatimids, Salah al-Din did not want a private royal fortified palace. Instead, he wanted a thriving metropolis where the people enjoyed commercial and cultural liberty. In place of the Fatimid monuments, al-Din built his own Islamic buildings. He continued the expansion of the City of the Dead as the main burial ground for Cairo and many tombs date from this era. Still, Ayyubid rule lasted a mere 75 years. Salah al-Din left Cairo in 1182 in order to fight the Crusaders and never returned, dying in Damascus, Syria in 1193. In Cairo, Salah al-Din was succeeded by his brother Adil who was unable to live up to Salah al-Din's established ability to rule and advance Egypt economically and militarily. In A.D. 1250, the Mamlukes, an army regiment of Turkish slaves that al-Din had created, effectively seized power from their former rulers.

The Mamluke era is characterized by unsurpassed achievement in the arts and in Islamic building. This achievement is evident in the splendor of Mamluke monuments scattered throughout the City of the Dead, particularly in the Northern Cemetery. The Mamlukes built massive monasteries and tombs covered with ornate surfaces. The *arabesques* (ornamental designs based on vegetal forms in which leaves and stems form a reciprocal, continuous interlacing pattern) and stone domes of the Mamlukes are considered unequalled in the Islamic world. Some of the best can be seen in the Northern Cemetery of the City of the Dead.

As in past eras, the Mamlukes did not use the City of the Dead as simply a burial ground. The cemeteries continued to be an active part of the overall community. The Northern Cemetery actually began as a hippodrome that hosted circus events and athletic competitions. In addition, Sufi monasteries and schools were built in the City of the Dead. Mamluke monasteries, largely self-sufficient, often housed such sophisticated facilities as rooms for travelers, mills, and bakeries.

In A.D. 1517, Egypt fell under the control of the Ottoman Empire. The most famous ruler of this period was Muhammad Ali, who massacred the last of the Mamlukes in 1811. Under the Ottoman Turks, the City of the Dead continued to be used and expanded. During this period, many of the older tombs and monuments of the cemeteries were restored and remodeled in Turkish style, of which evidence can still be seen throughout the City of the Dead. Still, the City of the Dead began to lose the importance in the community that it had attained during Mamluke rule. The hippodrome, Sufi monasteries, and Islamic schools that had once been such important parts of the community began to fall into disrepair.

In 1798, Napoleon Bonaparte ushered in a brief period of French occupation when he landed in Egypt with an army of soldiers and scientists, intent upon setting up a French colony in Egypt. Whereas the French never did establish complete control over Egypt, the French invasion further lessened the City of the Dead's role in society. Like Western society today, the French were of the opinion that cemeteries are for the dead and the dead only. People living in and carrying out other activities in the cemeteries began to be viewed as abnormal and their activities as sacrilegious. Still, the City of the Dead continued to grow and provide a refuge for those people with no other housing options.

The Western view that was introduced by the French regarding the strict purpose and use of the cemetery as a place only for the dead was reinforced by the subsequent British presence. Whereas a community of people still lived in the City of the Dead, the majority of Cairenes began to see the cemeteries as simply burial grounds – areas that should be kept segregated from the rest of the community. Physically, the City of the Dead had established its borders and the open spaces between the major monuments and tombs quickly began to fill in with modern tombs that were typically poorly built and lacked the artistic attributes of the earlier structures.

THE MODERN CITY OF THE DEAD

In the first half of the twentieth century, the City of the Dead would once again become a more active and important part of the community of Cairo. As the government of Egypt focused its efforts and finances on the World Wars, Cairo's infrastructure failed to grow at an adequate pace to provide affordable and decent housing to its expanding population. At the same time that construction of residential housing in Cairo was at a minimum, migrants from the countryside were trekking to Cairo in alarming numbers. Soon, Cairo had a housing crisis of alarming proportions. With no apparent alternative, many newcomers to Cairo, as well as some established urbanites (who became victims of Cairo's housing crisis), sought refuge in the cemeteries. Accounts show that by 1947 there were already some 50,000 people living in the City of the Dead. [8] With no relief in sight, the situation only got worse. People who had settled in the cemeteries as a temporary solution to their housing needs found it impossible to secure formal housing. Hence, their temporary shelter was becoming their permanent home. By 1960, the numbers of people living in the cemeteries had swelled to 80,000. One decade later, some 100,000 people were living in the City of the Dead. [9] To accommodate this growing community of tomb-dwellers, factories, stores, coffee shops, and other facilities also grew up among the tombs.

---

8   See Janet Abu-Lughod's Cairo: 1001 Years the City Victorious.

9   See Abu-Lughod

The Vast Metropolis of the City of the Dead

Many of Cairo's more traditional families still visit the cemeteries during religious festivals and on the birthdays of deceased relatives. Some families make weekly pilgrimages to the City of the Dead. Indeed, on Thursdays and Fridays, the cemeteries are teeming with women clothed in black *galabeyas* (long, flowing traditional robes). Some of these women bring food with them to prepare at the family tomb. This act of "picnicking with the dead" is a modern extension of the Pharaonic practice of leaving food at the tombs as an offering to the deceased with the belief that it will provide nourishment in the afterlife. People can also be seen burning incense in front of tombs or placing flowers as an offering to the deceased.

Cairenes also come to the City of the Dead for more festive occasions. There are various *moulids*, or religious festivals, that are held at different tombs across the cemeteries. These festivals are an interesting combination of both prayer and entertainment, attracting the religious, those just out to have fun, as well as the occasional foreigner in search of a cultural experience. There are also weekly markets in the City of the Dead that attract people from all across Cairo (See Chapter 6).

Many of the monuments of the cemeteries are highly revered among pious Muslims who make a vow to visit these sites before their death. It is not uncommon to see villagers from the Egyptian countryside or pilgrims from other Muslim countries arriving at the City of the Dead to visit these tombs in search of *baraka* (spiritual blessing) and religious fulfillment. The poor and the sick also seek refuge at these tombs in the hope of obtaining blessing from the deceased Islamic saints and to solicit alms from pilgrims to the tombs.

Today, the City of the Dead is home to more than 500,000 people [10] nestled between the centuries of history that the major monuments symbolize. It is a unique community in Cairo that represents Cairo's evolution and Islamic history as well as the profound development challenges that face Egypt in modern times.

ISLAMIC ART AND ARCHITECTURE

There are four basic types of Islamic structures described in this book: the mosque, the tomb/mausoleum, the *madrasa* (Islamic school), and the monastery. The following is a brief description of each type of building:

Mosque: A mosque is a place where Muslims gather to recite prayers while facing towards the holy city of Mecca in Saudi Arabia. A mosque can be as simple as a small carpeted building in an alleyway between two larger buildings in downtown Cairo or can be as elaborate as a multi-story structure covering acres of land and adorned with minarets, domes, arches, and intricate carvings.

---

10   Estimates of the population of the City of the Dead vary between 250,000 and one million.

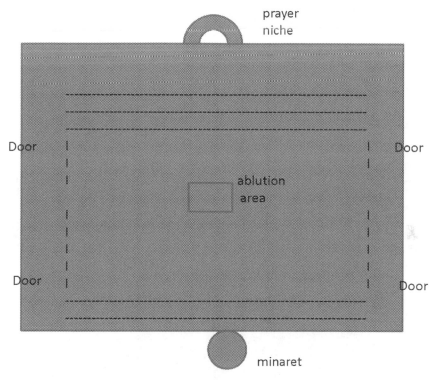

prayer
niche

Door

Door

ablution
area

Door

Door

minaret

Layout of Congregational Mosque

One common type of mosque is the congregational mosque. This type of mosque typically consists of a large square courtyard that is surrounded by aisles. Arcades (a series of arches supported by columns) separate the aisles from the courtyard. A *liwan* (a vaulted recessed room) is on the side of the courtyard facing Mecca and is larger than the other aisles in order to accommodate people praying.

Typical Prayer Niche

There are various components that make up a typical mosque. One wall of a mosque must face Mecca. This wall is called the *qibla* wall. In the center of this wall is a prayer niche (recess) or *mihrab* which indicates the direction of Mecca to mosque patrons and is typically the most decorated feature of the mosque. To the right of the mihrab, is typically a staircase leading to a small platform which serves as the *minbar* or pulpit from which sermons are delivered by an *imam*, the man who leads prayer in a mosque. In larger mosques, there is frequently a *dikka*, or raised platform where the ritual postures of the imam and responses are repeated so that the larger congregation can follow. Next to the dikka is typically a *kursi* which is a lectern where the Islamic holy book, the Qur'an, is placed.

Example of Minbar

Minarets tend to be the most readily recognizable part of a mosque. Traditionally, minarets were used to call Muslims to prayer at the mosque. Nowadays, this function is typically done by using a recorded call to prayer made through loud speakers, leaving the minarets as mainly symbolic.

Example of a Minaret

The doorway to a mosque is called a *portal*. Portals are often monumental and ornately decorated.

Example of a Portal

Tomb/Mausoleum: There are various types of Islamic tombs found in Cairo. As described earlier, Cairenes typically intern their dead in underground rooms that are built to accommodate entire families. The tombs traditionally have rooms and courtyards built above them to house the families of the deceased during visits. There are also underground tombs built for a single individual within a family tomb compound. These tombs typically have various types of markers or headstones. More elaborate tombs and mausoleums will have domed chambers with one or more tombs underneath.

Madrasa: The Islamic school was developed in Cairo with the first madrasa being constructed at the Mausoleum of the Imam al-Shafi'i, the founder of modern Islam (See Itinerary II). The school was built by Salah al-Din al-Ayyubi as part of his effort to return Egypt to the Sunni Islamic fold. A typical madrasa has an open courtyard surrounded by four liwans. In these liwans, the four rites of Sunni Islam were taught (Hanafi, Shafi'i, Wahabi and Maliki). In addition to the courtyard and liwans, there would be cells for students. This type of madrasa was popular in the early Mamluke period.

A second type of madrasa became popular in the late Mamluke era. This type was a smaller building than the earlier schools and consists of a covered courtyard, two large liwans, and two smaller liwans. This resulted in a more rectangular-shaped structure due to the fact that the living quarters were moved to independent buildings.

Monastery (Khanqah): A monastery is a residence for a community of people under religious vows. Under Mamluke rule, the Sufi sect of Islam became a state-sponsored institution and numerous monasteries were built in the City of the Dead to accommodate Sufi monks who sought to escape to the relative quiet of the cemeteries in order to lead lives of prayer and religious contemplation. These monastery complexes consisted of mosques, mausoleums, and madrasas in addition to cells for the Sufi monks.

STYLE AND GROWTH OF ISLAMIC ARCHITECTURE IN CAIRO

From the early Arab conquerors to the Ottoman Turks, each era of new leadership in Islamic Egypt brought with them innovative artistic and architectural developments.

Of note is the Islamic faith's ban on images of humans and of God in religious settings. Instead, Islam has substituted geometric designs such as arabesques to decorate its sacred buildings. These will be clearly visible throughout the monuments of the City of the Dead, regardless of the period that they were built. In addition, Islamic calligraphy was also used to decorate religious buildings.

The following is a brief look at some of the major achievements in art and architecture made during various periods of Islamic rule:

Post Arab Conquest (A.D. 640 – 969): This period pre-dates the founding of the city of al-Qahira. Monuments from this period were constructed when al-Fustat was Egypt's capital city. Some monuments still remain from this period but do not constitute a particular style. Instead, builders appear to have borrowed various styles and construction techniques from different parts of the Islamic world. These styles were combined with more traditional (pre-Islamic) Egyptian building practices.

Fatimids (A.D. 969-1175): The Fatimids introduced stone masonry to Egypt's architecture and built the earliest domes in Cairo. The Fatimids frequently used stucco work in their monuments and institutionalized the use of the keel arch in their walls, windows, minarets, and prayer niches. The Fatimids also introduced ribbing on domes as well as the use of stalactite ornamentation.

Example of arches

Ayyubids (A.D. 1175 – 1250): Ayyubid rule was brief and little architectural achievement was noted. The Ayyubids largely used and refined the architectural style of the Fatimids. The one highly notable creation of the Ayyubid period is the development of the madrasa or Islamic school as described above.

Early Mamluke (A.D. 1250 – 1350): Mamlukes are known for their achievements in art and architecture. As avid builders, Mamlukes constructed monuments throughout the City of the Dead. Much experimentation took place during the early Mamluke period. The cruciform madrasa was developed. Minarets were changed from being square-shaped to stylish octagonal and round structures. Mamlukes incorporated colored marble and mosaics in their structures and began to use red and white striped masonry (a style called *ablaq*) on the outside of their buildings. The early Mamluke period was also characterized by ribbed domes, pointed arches and monumental doorways decorated with a stalactite motif.

Example of Dome and Support

Late Mamluke (A.D. 1430 – 1517): The major development during this period was the stone dome. Also, stone carving reached its height of achievement during the late Mamluke period as the surfaces of domes and minarets were intricately carved with geometric and arabesque designs. In addition, Mamluke decorative arts such as

21

enameled and gilded glass, inlaid metalwork and textiles were prized in international trade of the period.

Ottoman Turks (A.D. 1517 – 1798): Under Ottoman rule, more emphasis was put on the construction of secular buildings than of religious buildings. Still, a few developments in religious and funerary architecture were made during this period. The traditional congregational mosque was modified so that the sanctuary was enclosed and covered with a dome. In addition, the size and importance of the aisles were reduced. Also, minarets became more simple structures than the elaborately carved minarets of the Mamlukes. Ottoman minarets are long, cylinder-like structures with tapered tops (shaped something like a sharpened pencil).

TIPS FOR VISITORS

- There are many important Islamic monuments for visitors to see in the City of the Dead that are spread across the various cemeteries. With significant distance separating many monuments, visitors should expect to do some serious walking. Therefore, comfortable shoes should be worn.

- Visitors should remember that these Muslim cemeteries are areas of religious significance. Respect for the religious traditions and customs of Egyptian Muslims should be considered at all times. Conservative and deferential behavior should be shown inside the Islamic monuments and both men and women should dress appropriately by choosing modest clothing. Visitors wearing shorts or short skirts and dresses, sleeveless blouses, etc. may not be allowed to enter some monuments (especially mosques). Revealing tops should also be avoided and it is customary for women to have their arms and hair covered.

- Many of the monuments are under the supervision of the Egyptian Antiquities Organization and a small entrance fee will be charged. This fee usually ranges between 6 and 20 Egyptian pounds (LE). Rates for Egyptian nationals are considerably cheaper (usually .5 LE or 1 LE). Visitors with student identification cards or diplomatic identification cards will typically be able to enter at a discount, normally fifty percent. At some monuments, an additional fee may be charged for picture taking or the use of video recorders. Fees will be paid to a care-taker. These care-takers will frequently offer to guide visitors, offering simple explanations on the various parts and functions of the building. Care-takers may also offer to guide visitors to areas that are generally restricted access or may offer to perform the call to prayer. For these services, care-takers will expect to receive *baksheesh* (tips)[11]. A typical tip is 1 or 2 LE. If the care-taker has performed a special service (such as performing the call to prayer), a larger tip of LE 5 will be appreciated. It is advisable for visitors to the City of the Dead to go to a bank or exchange office prior to their visit to the cemeteries and get sufficient small change (LE 1 and LE 5 notes) in order to pay for admission tickets and *backsheesh*. Oftentimes, no change will be available at the monuments themselves so it is better to have the exact amounts that you need.

• Out of respect, Egyptian Muslims remove their shoes before entering a mosque to pray. Visitors to mosques in the City of the Dead must adhere to this tradition. At some mosques, shoe covers will be provided to visitors. These are typically made of burlap, slip over your shoes and tie at the back. These prevent the bottom of your shoes which have been dirtied from walking in unclean places from touching the floor of the holy building. At other mosques, visitors will be asked to remove their shoes

---

11 The simple definition of *backsheesh* is tips. To fully understand the concept of backsheesh, however, requires further explanation as there are various types of backsheesh. Backsheesh can mean tipping for services rendered. This type of tipping goes beyond what is normal in the West and may include a bathroom attendant, someone who opens a door for you or the person who puts your bag through security at the airport. Another type of backsheesh is that given for the granting of favors. For example, if a tomb of the City of the Dead is closed to the general public, a small tip will more often than not produce the key. The final type of backsheesh is alms giving. Giving alms to the poor is a tenant of Islam and visitors of the City of the Dead may experience requests for this type of backsheesh when visiting tombs of revered Islamic saints such as Sayyida Nafisa or the Imam al-Shafi'i.

entirely. Therefore, it is advisable to wear heavy socks, especially in the winter months when stone or tile floors get quite cold. Sometimes there is a shoe rack where your shoes can be left. At other times, you must carry your shoes throughout your visit. If this is the case, you should carry your shoes so that the soles are facing each other as in Egypt, showing someone the bottom of your shoes is a sign of disrespect.

- Many of the mosques in the City of the Dead are working mosques. Therefore, it is best to plan your visit around prayer times, especially on Fridays when communal prayers are more popular and services tend to be longer. Prayer times change with the seasons and are listed in the local newspapers.

- Visitors who wish to climb to the top of minarets of mosques (when this is allowable) should bring a small flashlight with them as it is typically very dark inside the stairways of the minarets and steps may be worn or broken.

- When walking between monuments, visitors must remember that they are not merely walking in a cemetery. Rather, the City of the Dead is an inhabited community. The hordes of children that may be attracted by your presence in their world will remind you that the cemeteries provide informal housing for some 500,000 of Egypt's urban poor. Children will typically ask for money or pens. Visitors who bring pens and change with them to give away will be rewarded with the smiles of the cemeteries' children. At times, the children can be very persistent. This is due to the belief among many traditional Egyptians that the more fortunate should give to those less advantaged.

- At some mosques (especially the mosque of Sayyida Nafisa [see Itinerary I]), groups of poor and sick will gather outside in order to solicit alms from pilgrims and other visitors. Expect to be approached and solicited for money. Choosing to give or not to give is the individual decision of each visitor. This author suggests, however, that if there is a group of solicitors, visitors may want to refrain from giving. Typically, if one person is given money, the visitor is surrounded by the entire group demanding alms for each individual. At these times, the solicitors can be quite persistent and may even grab the arm of a visitor who attempts to walk away. Reciting the phrase "rabii adeekak" or "God will give to you" usually has a calming effect.

- Visitors will encounter women sitting in doorways of tomb-homes, shopkeepers, people walking to work, men sitting in the cemeteries' coffee houses and women and children fetching water and carrying out other chores. At times, it can actually be easy to forget that you are in a cemetery. Expect the people of the City of the Dead to be friendly and as curious of you as you are of them. Do not expect to meet any hostility. In fact, visitors may be invited to share a cup of tea with a family in their tomb-home. If such an opportunity arises, take advantage of it. In most cases, the people will be honored to host you and will expect nothing in return. The Northern Cemetery is visited more frequently by tourists than other areas of the City of the Dead. People there will be less interested in your presence in their community. In other areas of the cemeteries, foreigners wondering among the tombs may bring residents to the doors and windows of their tomb-homes. Visitors may be asked where they are headed or what they are looking for.

- Visitors should feel free to take pictures of the monuments. If one wishes to take pictures of the City of the Dead's residents, however - especially of women - it is advisable to first ask for permission (see *Commonly Used Arabic Phrases*). Traditional Egyptians do not always appreciate having their photographs taken by strangers. Children will often be more willing to allow their pictures to be taken and may even encourage a visitor with a camera. A small tip of a pen or change will likely be expected.

- Many visitors to the City of the Dead fear crime. In fact, there is a long association of crime with the cemeteries of the City of the Dead. Indeed, the cemeteries are said to have once been a popular refuge for criminals hiding from the law. The cemetery community, however, is not a dangerous place. Still, the same precautions that a visitor to a foreign place would normally take apply. Visitors unfamiliar with the City of the Dead should visit during daylight hours when the people of the community are busy carrying out their daily tasks and the streets are populated. Avoid wearing excessive jewelry or expensive clothing and shy away from any confrontational situations that arise. Most of all, demonstrate respect for the people of this unique community. If one does this, a visit to the City of the Dead will be both enjoyable and rewarding.

HOW TO USE THIS GUIDE

This guide provides itineraries for four walking tours of the City of the Dead that can be done separately in order to accommodate visitors with little time, or which can be combined to present a more encompassing view of the cemetery communities. Visitors with little time are recommended to tour the Northern Cemetery (Itinerary IV) first as it is home to some of the most impressive monuments of the Islamic world. Each walking tour has a starting point and an end point as well as an estimate of the amount of time needed to complete the tour. In addition, each itinerary has a map that shows the route to be taken as well as several photographs, illustrations, and ground plans of monuments to be visited. The last chapter looks at the markets and festivals that take place in the City of the Dead at various times of the year.

The monuments in the itineraries have been chosen for their beauty and historical importance. The entry for each monument contains three sections: *History* – this section offers an explanation of the historical importance of the monument and/or the person(s) for whom the monument was built; *Description* – this segment will walk a visitor through a monument and will point out its major architectural and artistic features; and *Access for Visitors* – this part describes the accessibility of the different monuments to the general public (at some monuments, access may be restricted to Muslims or men may be allowed into some areas that women are not). The tours will guide the visitor through the monument step-by-step, room-by-room, explaining the main components of the buildings and their importance. Chapter six is not a walking tour but a chance for visitors to the cemeteries to take a look at modern life in the City of the Dead. This chapter provides information on the locations and times of the various markets and religious festivals that take place in the City of the Dead.

So, put on your comfortable walking shoes and get started.....

CHAPTER 2
Itinerary I: The Cemetery of the Great

Featured Monuments:

- *Mosque and Mausoleum of*
- *Sayyida Nafisa*
- *Tomb of the Abbasid Caliphs*
- *Tomb of Sayyida Ruqayya*
- *Tombs of Sayyida ʿAttika and*
- *Mohamed al-Gafari*
- *Tomb of Shagar al-Durr*

Estimated Time: 2 hours

Where to start?: The Cemetery of the Great is south of the Citadel and on the Nile side of Salah Salem Highway, ending where the highway and the ancient aqueduct that once supplied water to the Citadel turn westward toward the Nile. To get there, drive south on Salah Salem from the Citadel. The cemetery will soon be to the right and the aqueduct to the left. At the point where the aqueduct turns toward the Nile, a driver has the option of continuing straight or turning right alongside the aqueduct. Turn right. As you turn the corner, there will be another right hand turn that heads into the cemetery. Take this street and continue straight to a fairly large square with a large round garden and a mosque on the right side. This is the Sayidda Nafisa Mosque and Mausoleum and is the starting point for Itinerary One.

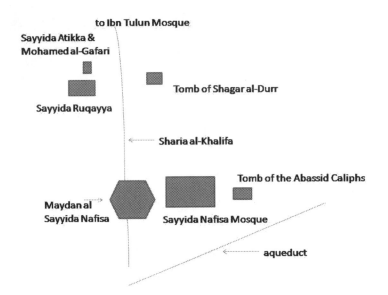

Map of the Cemetery of the Great

MOSQUE AND MAUSOLEUM OF SAYYIDA NAFISA

History

The Mosque and Mausoleum of Sayyida Nafisa is one of the most beloved and popular shrines in the City of the Dead. Sayyida Nafisa was the granddaughter of al-Hasan, the grandson of the Prophet Muhammed. She was born in the year 145 of the Islamic calendar[12]. Born in Mecca, Nafisa spent the greater part of her childhood in Medina and Monawara, Arabia. At a very young age, she memorized the entire Qur'an and studied Islamic jurisprudence. Indeed, Nafisa would become known as a *hafizat al-Qur'an* or, "one who knows the Qur'an by heart".

---

12 The Islamic calendar (or Hijri calendar) is a purely lunar calendar. It contains 12 months that are based on the motion of the moon, and because 12 synodic months is only 12 x 29.53=354.36 days, the Islamic calendar is consistently shorter than a tropical year, and therefore it shifts with respect to the Christian calendar.

Nafisa participated in praying the five daily prayers regularly from the age of six and became renowned for her piety, fasting, praying throughout the night and for devotion to the worship of God. In her lifetime, Nafisa would perform the hajj (pilgrimage to Mecca) some thirty times.

At the age of sixteen, Nafisa married Isaac ibn Jaffar and gave birth to two children, a son and a daughter. She and her husband traveled to Egypt in the seventh century and stayed with her cousin, known as the Lady Sakina. She later lived in a house in the area of what is her present-day mosque. She became known as a pious Muslim and would recite the traditions of the Prophet Muhammad. Locals felt that Nafisa possessed *baraka*, or spiritual blessing. From distant corners of Egypt, people came to visit Nafisa and be blessed by her. Nafisa was so popular that, at one point, the huge gatherings of people became such a burden on Nafisa that she could not observe her daily recitations and decided to leave Egypt. Egyptians appealed to the Governor of Egypt who asked Nafisa to stay. She agreed on the condition that she would receive people only on Saturdays and Wednesdays and the remaining days were devoted to her private worship of God.

The Imam al-Shafi'I (See Itinerary II), founder of one of the four rites of Sunni Islam, lived near Sayyida Nafisa and would visit her to collect traditions of the Prophet. When al-Shafi'i was sick, he would send one of his students to sit with Nafisa and learn from her. Nafisa would pray for the health of al-Shafi'i and sometimes, by the time the student had returned, al-Shafi'i would miraculously be back in good health. One time, however, Nafisa sent the student back with a message for al-Shafi'i stating that God would lift him to His proximity. Al-Shafi'i soon died. Fulfilling al-Shafi'i's wishes, his body was brought before Nafisa upon his death and she recited the funeral prayers over him.

Nafisa is credited with some 150 miracles. One of most popular stories about miracles attributed to Sayyida Nafisa happened shortly after her arrival in Egypt. A non-Muslim neighbor left their paralyzed daughter at Nafisa's house while running out to do some chores. As Nafisa washed herself in preparation for prayers, the water flowed off of Nafisa and touched the girl. The young girl rubbed the water on her feet and legs and was then able to stand. The girl's family became believers in Islam after this miracle.

Legend claims that - as Nafisa felt her own death approaching - she fasted and dug her own grave inside her house. She prayed there until she died in A.D. 824. A shrine was built over her tomb. This was later expanded into a mosque. These structures have been enlarged and rebuilt many times. In fact, nothing remains of the original buildings. It is believed, however, that this area of the cemetery was built up around her tomb as people sought to be buried beside and live near Nafisa, now considered to be a Muslim saint. Indeed, given Nafisa's reputation for baraka and her good deeds, people chose to be buried around her mosque and tomb in order to receive her blessings. Religion Professor Valerie J. Hoffman explains that, "Throughout the Muslim world, the presence of saints has been a source of comfort to people. The mere presence of a saint's tomb in the neighbourhood is thought to confer blessings, protection and prosperity." [13]

The present-day mosque of Sayyida Nafisa is a place of constant activity. Typically, numerous marriages are performed at the mosque each week, making the mosque one of the most popular places in Cairo to get married. Couples wed in Sayyida Nafisa mosque with the belief that her blessing will make their marriage strong and long-lasting. The area around this mosque and mausoleum has been an active part of Cairo since the days of Sayyida Nafisa and continues to be one of the most urbanized areas of the City of the Dead. While visiting the mosque and mausoleum of Sayyida Nafisa, the devotion of Egyptians to this Muslim saint is readily apparent.

---

13   Hoffman, Valerie E., "Saints and Sheikhs in Modern Egypt, Regional Issues Egypt at http://www.isim.nl/newsletter/2/regional/11.html.

Description

Nothing is left of the original structure of what was Sayyida Nafisa's home and later, mosque and mausoleum. The present structure dates to 1897 and was built after a fire had significantly damaged the older structure. The large, newer façade and courtyard of the mosque was begun by the Egyptian Government in late 1997 and was completed in 1998.

To enter the building, proceed down the alleyway on the left hand side of the mosque. Follow the wall of the mosque on your right passing a small coffee shop and some vendors of the informal economy until you reach a doorway at the very back of the building. This is the entrance. Pass through the doorway and you will find a care-taker who will ask you to remove your shoes. Ahead, you will find two doors: one directly behind where the care-taker is overseeing the shoes and an additional door off to the left. Women are allowed access to only certain areas of the complex and must proceed through the left door. Men enter through the door to the right.

Women enter directly into the tomb area. Men enter the mosque first and then can enter the tomb area through a doorway on the wall to the left. In the tomb chamber, a *mashrabiya*[14] screen separates the men's viewing areas from the women's. When entering the room, notice the large wooden doors with elaborate metalwork. At the center of the room is the cenotaph[15] of Saint Sayyida Nafisa. The cenotaph is covered with a black cloth that is decorated with calligraphy from the Qur'an in white. Lacework is also used as decoration and there is a Qur'an housed in a beautiful mother-of-pearl case. Four brass posts grace the corners of the cenotaph.

---

14 Mashrabiya was originally a place for drinking but is commonly used to designate windows or grills with latticed work screen of turned or carved wood. Mashrabiya were a hallmark of Islamic domestic architecture. These windows provided protection from the sunrays and offered privacy to women from passers-by.

15 A cenotaph is a symbolic tomb that honors the dead but does not actually contain the body.

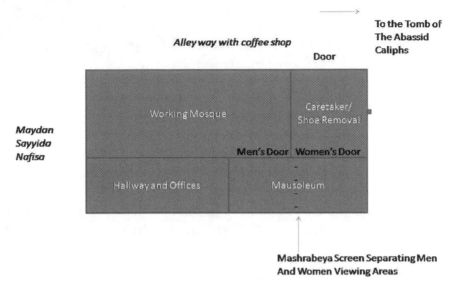

Floor Plan of Sayyida Nafisa Mosque

The cenotaph is inside a glass structure with bronze caging. This structure is topped with a small dome. Look above this structure and the larger dome of the tomb chamber is visible. At almost any time of the day, it is common to see men and women sitting in the tomb chamber praying to Sayyida Nafisa to fulfill various types of favors. If you look above her grave, Nafisa's lineage to the Prophet is engraved there as well as a statement saying that anyone experiencing difficulties in life should visit Nafisa's grave, recite Islamic prayers and allow God to solve their problems.

Women visitors must exit the same door that they entered through and are not allowed in the main mosque area. Men can exit the tomb chamber through a door on the left side. This exit leads into a hallway where there are various offices. Of primary interest in this hallway, however, are the wall hangings that are found on the right-hand side. There is a very large and old piece of embroidery in red, black and yellow that bears the names (in Arabic calligraphy) of the four caliphs (successors to the Prophet). In addition, there is a framed document that gives the life history of Sayyida Nafisa, also in Arabic.

Exit the hallway at the opposite end and you will enter the mosque. It quickly becomes apparent that this large mosque was built over the course of different periods. The room that you have entered is significantly older than the room beyond. In this older section, notice the attractive tile mihrabs *(prayer niches)* and the wooden minbar (pulpit). The ceiling is made of painted wood and is held up by attractive marble columns.

In the newer section of the mosque, the ceiling is made of plaster and bears eye-catching paintings of geometric designs and flower motifs. Marble columns provide support. In both areas, the floor is covered with oriental carpets and chandeliers provide light.

Access to Visitors

Non-Muslims are allowed to visit the mausoleum of Sayyida Nafisa. Only men, however, are allowed inside the mosque -- an active place of worship and a place of constant activity. Lucky visitors to Sayyida Nafisa may also be able to get themselves invited to one of the many weddings that take place there each week. First, find out if a wedding is scheduled (workers at the neighboring coffee shop on the right side of the mosque entrance usually know). Wait outside of the mosque at the scheduled time and you will likely be invited to participate in the festivities. If you are male, you will be escorted to a room upstairs where you can witness the marriage agreement between the groom and the father-of-the-bride in the presence of the *meuzziun* (Islamic religious authority who conducts marriages). Female visitors must wait outside with the rest of the women until the groom and the father-of-the-bride have joined hands in agreement and a celebration begins.

THE TOMB OF THE ABBASID CALIPHS

From Sayyida Nafisa, return to the passageway along the left side of the mosque. Continue down the passageway walking away from the main square of Sayyida Nafisa. At the end of the passageway, pass through a doorway followed by a covered passageway. After a few feet, there will be an alleyway on your right that leads to the Tomb of the Abbasid Caliphs.

History

Among the monuments of the cemeteries bearing evidence to Ayyubid rule (A.D. 1171 – 1250) is the tomb of the Abbasid Caliphs. During the height of their power, the Abbasid Caliphs ruled the entire Muslim Empire with the exception of Spain. As their rule was declining, the Abbasid Caliphs were driven from Baghdad by the Mongols. They accepted an offer from the Mamluke Sultan Baybars to be reestablished in Cairo. Later, in 1517, the last Abbasid Caliph was formally divested of his office. In 1538, the Ottomans assumed the Caliphate until it was abolished in the 1920s by Ataturk, the founder of modern Turkey.

The tomb of the Abbasid Caliphs was constructed in A.D. 1242 by a man named Abu Nadla who served as ambassador to Egypt from the Abbasid Caliphate in Baghdad. When the Abbasid Caliphs came to Cairo in 1261, they found the tomb Abu Nadla had built and took it for themselves. The tomb is located directly behind Sayyida Nafisa's Mosque. The Caliphs enlarged the tomb to include ample room for the traditional celebrations for the dead and added accommodations for a tomb keeper. This important mausoleum now contains seventeen tombs, including wooden cenotaphs for Abu Nadla, the sons of the Sultan Baybars and numerous men and women from the Abbasid family (including the fourth and sixth Caliphs). As in the case with other monuments of the City of the Dead (such as the Mausoleum of the Imam al-Shafi'i), the original *mihrabs* of this complex were not correctly oriented with the holy city of Mecca. As a result, corrections were made and there are now seven *mihrabs* in the tomb.

Description

This small building is dwarfed by Sayydia Nafisa's mosque and mausoleum but is still impressive in its simplicity. It is covered by a brick and cement dome that lacks decoration. The dome sits on a base with steps at the four corners. There are three windows in simple Ayyubid style: the top window is an elongated rectangle with a triangle on each end. The two lower windows have half of this shape. These keel-arched windows are the second earliest example in Egypt of stucco window grills with a floral arabesque design and with glass still intact. The façade of the building has three keel-shaped arcades carved into the plaster. The arches are decorated with ribs and have beveled corners. The middle arch contains the doorway to the tomb.

Inside of the tomb there are eight cenotaphs belonging to the children of the Abbasid Caliphs, to Abu Nadla, and to the sons of the Sultan Baybars. There are also epitaphs (inscriptions) on the walls for seventeen members of the Abbasid family. Be sure to inspect the main prayer niche. It is constructed in typical Fatimid style and has fine stucco carving and painted *Kufic* (Islamic calligraphy) inscriptions. In the center, there is a medallion with lines radiating out from it. Also, the interior of the dome boasts of impressive carved stucco and painted medallions.

Access to Visitors

This tomb is kept locked by the Egyptian Antiquities Organization. Ask the locals, however, and someone may produce a key. Recent visitors to the tomb, however, have been advised by locals that only the Egyptian Antiquities Organization has access (this was the situation in March 2005). In any case, it is worth the effort to ask and to visit the outside of the tomb.

THE TOMB OF SAYYIDA RUQAYYA

From the tomb of the Abbasid Caliphs, return to the square in front of Sayyida Nafisa's mosque. Walk up the street leading northwards from the square (towards the Citadel). This is Khalifa Street (Sharia Khalifa). After a few hundred feet, you will see a ribbed dome on the left next to the road and two smaller plain domes about 35 farther feet away and set in from the street. In between there is an entryway. Typically, there are people gathered at the entrance. This is the entrance to a tomb complex that includes the Tomb of Sayyida Ruqayya. Enter the complex and Ruqayya's tomb will be on your left. [16]

History

Sayyida Ruqayya was the daughter of 'Ali, the fourth Caliph and the husband of the Prophet's daughter Fatima. Ruqayya was not, however, the daughter of Fatima. Rather, she was Ali's daughter from another wife. Ruqayya came to Cairo with her step-sister Zaynab. Along with Sayyida Nafisa, Ruqayya and Zaynab are considered to be the patron saints of the city of Cairo. Although Ruqayya is actually buried in Damascus, Syria, a shrine was built in Cairo in A.D. 1133 by the wife of the Fatimid Caliph al-Amir. The shrine is a place where pilgrims come to make vows and to pray for the saint's intercession.

Description

Enter the compound through the green and white doorway and proceed down the walkway. At the end of the walkway on your left will be the entrance to Sayyida Ruqayya's small complex. Remove your shoes here and give them to the care-taker. In front of you are two courtyards: one raised and one lowered. Frequently, men will be found lounging and praying in these courtyards. The lower courtyard has a few cenotaphs of distant relatives of the Prophet Muhammad.

---

16   In March 2005, there was a significant amount of rubble near the entryway where a building and wall had been torn down.

Years ago, there were many more cenotaphs and grave stones in this area.[17] The care taker will tell you, however, that most of these were removed to other areas of the cemetery by Shi'ite Muslims from India who wished to preserve this area solely for members of the Prophet's family.

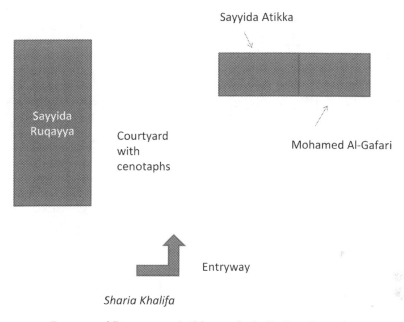

Layout of Ruqayya, Atikka and al-Gafari Complex

Beyond the lower courtyard is a small building -- the tomb chamber of Sayyida Ruqayya. This building is modest in size but is handsomely decorated and attracts pilgrims from throughout the Muslim world. Enter inside and you will be immediately struck by the poor restoration work that has been done, much of which appears simply to consist of new plaster hastily applied on decaying walls. Still, some of the beauty of the original work can be detected. Fragments of the ribbing of the dome and its stalactite support system are still preserved and there are three *mihrabs* (prayer niches) that are among

---

17 Other accounts claim that these cenotaphs belong to restorers and patrons of the eighteenth century (See Parker, Sabin & Williams, Islamic Monuments in Cairo, page 135).

the few remaining in Egypt from the Fatimid era. These mihrabs are in bad condition but still have impressive columns built at their sides as well as splendid keel-shaped arches. The middle prayer niche has a unique feature: in the center of the niche is the name of 'Ali surrounded by the name of Muhammed. The name of the Prophet is repeated seven times. As mentioned earlier, Fatimids were Shi'ite Muslims who believed that 'Ali was Muhammad's proper successor. The mausoleum had also contained a valuable wooden mihrab that has since been placed in the Islamic Art Museum in Cairo.

The wooden cenotaph of Sayyida Ruqayya is in the center of the room, covered with green and blue cloth. A stela rises at one end and is covered by lace. The tomb is usually adorned with silk flowers and one can smell the scent of perfume left behind by pilgrims. In addition, there is a small Qur'an on a stand as well as a set of prayer beads.

The cenotaph is surrounded by a metal screen or cage. The metal is molded to appear in the shape of mashrabeya and is decorated with verses from the Qur'an and a woven flower pattern.

Access to Visitors

Visitors are welcome and frequently make a pilgrimage to this tomb. There is no entrance fee but the care-taker will appreciate a small tip upon your departure.

THE TOMB OF SAYYIDA ATIKKA & MOHAMED AL-GAFARI

Step outside of Sayyida Ruqayya's tomb (remaining inside of the compound) and stand at the entrance of the courtyard. There will be a rectangular building directly in front of you. This building contains the tombs of Sayyida 'Attika and Mohamed al-Gafari.

Mohamed Al-Gafari Tomb Chamber

History

Among the most significant existing monuments of the Fatimid period are the tombs of Sayyida 'Atikka (A.D. 1122) and Mohamed al-Gafari (A.D. 1120), members of the family of the Prophet Muhammad. Al-Gafari was the great-great-great grandson of the Prophet. 'Atikka was an aunt of the Prophet. Muslims from throughout the Islamic world make a pilgrimage to this important burial ground, the largest related group of surviving funerary monuments from the first six centuries of Islam. The tombs are maintained by the Bohras, an Isma'li Shi'ite sub-sect located in India.

Description

The tomb chambers are small rooms with 'Atikka's chamber added onto al-Gafari's mausoleum. These two tombs are simply decorated but still contain fine stucco work as well as beautiful *kufic* (the earliest style of Arabic script) inscriptions. Enter al-Gafari's mausoleum first. It is quickly apparent that there has been some restoration work done in recent years. As with Ruqayya's tomb, efforts at restoration have been rough and unimpressive. The prayer niche consists of an unpainted cement recess in the wall. The dome is equally unimpressive. What is interesting about this tomb and the neighboring tomb of 'Atikka, however, is the evidence of the evolution of the dome support. In these tombs, a support that placed one niche over three niches (side by side) was used. This development was a bridge between the simple Fatimid support systems and the more elaborate support systems later used by the Mamlukes.

The cenotaph of al-Gafari is wooden and is covered over by a piece of green velvet cloth. A stela marks the position of the head.

Leave al-Gafari's tomb chamber and enter the adjoining tomb chamber of Sayyida 'Atikka. This chamber is very similar to al-Gafari's but more of the original work is intact. One can still see original ribbing on the dome as well as a strip of Islamic calligraphy across the base of the dome. Again, the cenotaph is covered with green velvet cloth.

Access to Visitors

As with Ruqayya's tomb, the tombs of Sayyida 'Atikka and Mohamed al-Gafari are open to visitors without any entrance fee. The care-taker is the same person as Sayyida Ruqayya's tomb. Therefore, if you tipped at Ruqayya's tomb there should be no pressure for additional tips to be given. Be careful to respect the tombs and their importance. Even in the absence of the care-taker, visitors should remember to remove their shoes at the doors of the tomb chambers.

THE TOMB OF SHAGAR AL-DURR

Leave the tomb complex of Ruqayya, 'Atikka, and al-Gafari and return to Khalifa Street. Across the road and to the left you will see a small tomb surrounded by a black, wrought iron fence. This is the tomb of Shagar al-Durr.

History

Shagar al-Durr's life was both interesting and unique. The Armenian slave wife of the last male ruler of the Ayyubid Dynasty, Shagar al-Durr was the sole female to rule during Islamic Egypt's lengthy history. Al-Salih Nagm al-Din, Shagar al-Durr's husband, died in A.D. 1224 while preparing for battle with the Crusaders. Cleverly, Shagar al-Durr concealed her husband's death for three months to allow his son, Turan Shah, to return to Egypt from Mesopotamia and inherit the throne.

During this period of concealment, the Mamlukes, an army regiment of Turkish slaves created by Salah al-Din, defeated the Crusaders at the "Battle of Mansoura". Rather than gratitude for their defense of the Ayyubid Kingdom, the Mamlukes received only ridicule from Turan Shah upon his return. Feeling disgraced, Shagar al-Durr conspired with the Mamluke generals to assassinate her step-son.

After the assassination, Shagar al-Durr proclaimed herself queen and ruled in Turan Shah's name for eighty days. Shagar al-Durr was the first female ruler to have coins struck and the Friday sermon pronounced in her name. The phenomenon of female rule, however, proved too incredible for Islamic Egypt of that period as well as for the Abbasid Caliph in Baghdad. Shagar al-Durr was thus forced into a marriage with Aybak, a Mamluke general (who is said to have been her lover), effectively passing power to a new dynasty. Still, for all intents and purposes, Shagar al-Durr maintained control.

Shagar al-Durr refused to hand over the throne's treasury to her new husband and their co-rule fell into jeopardy. In defiance, on April 29, 1257, Shagar al-Durr had Aybak murdered by her eunuchs as he walked into the palace baths. Her actions were avenged by those loyal to Aybak. She was arrested by the Mamlukes and imprisoned in the Red Tower of the Citadel. There, she was beaten to death and her body is said to have been cast from the tower of the Citadel to dogs waiting below. The body was retrieved and laid to rest in the Cemetery of the Great in a tomb she had ordered to be constructed during her rule.

Another version of the story of Shagar al-Durr's fall from power and her ultimate death claims that the conflict began when Aybak took a second wife. Furious, Shagar al-Durr had Aybak murdered and his second wife imprisoned. This act was avenged by Mamlukes loyal to Aybak who had Shagar al-Durr arrested. She was then beaten to death with wooden clogs by Aybak's second wife and other women. Her body was then hung off a tower of the Citadel where dogs were waiting to devour it.

Whereas it is not entirely clear which legend is correct, what is clear is that Shagar al-Durr's life was unprecedented in the history of Egypt and Islam and, with her death, ended another era in Cairo's history -- an era preserved in the mausoleums of the City of the Dead.

Description

This tomb is the last Ayyubid building to be constructed in Cairo (A.D. 1250). It is a small structure that is actually a combination of Fatimid and Ayyubid styles. Sitting below the current level of the street, the tomb is made of brick covered with plaster and carved with various decorations. Enter the courtyard through a gate at the beginning of the wrought iron fence. Before descending to the courtyard, take time to appreciate the structure from the outside. It is simple but elegant with a plain dome and supports and windows that are typical of the period.

Inside, the main object of importance is the prayer niche. This niche is unique in that it has a glass and mother-of-pearl mosaic. This mosaic is similar in style to Byzantine mosaics and may indicate influence from Syria. The mosaic shows the so-called 'tree of life'. The use of mother-of-pearl in the design is probably a play on the meaning of Shagar al-Durr's name, "Tree of Pearls".

The Tomb of Shagar al-Durr

Access to Visitors

This tomb is kept locked. A neighborhood man, however, has the key and will open the tomb for backsheesh (tips). Returning the way that you approached, there is a small coffee shop on the left. Beside the coffee shop is a small tomb painted green and white that is at the corner of a building. Ask for the person with the key here. [18]

---

18 In March 2005, this tomb complex was in disarray as garbage was strewn across the grounds. Scaffolding at the entrance to the tomb gave hope that restoration work is to be completed.

CHAPTER 3
Itinerary II: The Southern Cemetery

Featured Monuments:

- *Mosque and Mausoleum of the*
- *Imam*
- *Al-Shafi'i*
- *Howsh Al-Pasha*

Estimated Time: 1 hours and 15 minutes

Where to start?: The Southern Cemetery is wedged between Salah Salem Highway and the Moquattam Hills. It stretches lengthwise from the southeastern edge of the Citadel towards the suburb of Maadi. To get there travel down Salah Salem south from the Citadel. Go under the first bridge that passes over a crossing street. This is Sayyida Aisha Square. Turn under the bridge and drive straight into the cemetery. Drive down this curved street until you can go no further. On your right is a large mosque. This is the Mosque and Mausoleum of the Imam Al-Shafi'i and marks the beginning of itinerary two.

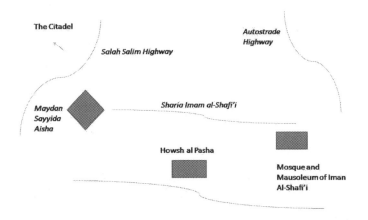

Map of the Southern Cemetery

THE MOSQUE AND MAUSOLEUM
OF THE IMAM AL-SHAFI'I

History

The Imam al-Shafi'i was the founder of one of the four rites of Sunni Islam and claimed descent from Abu Talib, the uncle of the Prophet Muhammed. He was born in Syria in A.D. 767 and was from the *Quarysh* (the tribe of the Prophet Muhammad in Arabia). His childhood was spent in poverty. He studied in Medina and traveled to Yemen where he was active in a rebellion that brought him into disfavor with the Caliph Hawn al-Rachid. He later taught in Baghdad, where he developed ideas on Islamic jurisprudence that would become the Shafi'ite rite of Islam to which most Egyptians and East African Muslims adhere to today. Cairo historian Gaston Wiet claims, "the role that he [the Imam al-Shafi'i] played in elaborating religious law is so important that it cannot be exaggerated, for he was truly the founder of methodology in the field of religious legislation."[19] He eventually traveled to Egypt, where he lived until his death.

Although the Imam al-Shafi'i died in Egypt in A.D. 820, the present foundation of his tomb dates to A.D. 1211. It is the largest detached Muslim tomb chamber in Egypt and was the first officially sponsored mausoleum to be built for a Sunni theologian following the overthrow of the Shi'ite Fatimids in 1171. The Imam was buried in the tomb area of the family of Sayyid Mohamed 'Abd al-Hakam. The mausoleum was built by al-Adil, brother of the famous Ayyubid leader Salah al-Din, and includes the 'Abd al-Hakam family cemetery within its walls.

Like other tombs in this area, al-Shafi'i's original mausoleum may have been a more simple burial chamber than the present-day structure. Over the centuries, however, more elaborate mausoleums were built over many of the older tombs, some even containing mosques and Islamic schools (*madrasa* in Arabic). The first of such schools in Egypt was founded by Salah al-Din al Ayyubi and was built at the Shafi'i burial site. Salah al-Din, founder of the Ayyubid Dynasty in twelfth century Egypt, built the school as part of his campaign to convert Egypt back from Shi'i Islam to Sunni Islam. Much like the Imam al-Shafi'i, he was a pioneer in Islamic education. His influence, too, can be seen throughout the City of the Dead's monuments.

---

19 Gaston Weit (translation by Seymour Feiler), <u>Cairo: City of Art and Commerce</u>, University of Oklahoma Press, Norman,, Oklahoma, 1964, P.13.

Dome of the Iman al-Shafi'I Mosque

In Sunni Islam, the Imam al-Shafi'i is esteemed as one of the great Muslim saints. As one of the City of the Dead's holiest shrines, it attracts visitors from around the Muslim world who make *ziyyarah*, or visitation, to the tomb to recite prayers in al-Shafi'i's honor. Every year, on the occasion of his birthday, a religious fair (*moulid*) is held at the tomb. It is one of the most popular religious celebrations in Cairo (see Chapter 5).

The Imam al-Shaffi's tomb is important in understanding the growth of the City of the Dead both physically and as an active part of the growing Muslim community of Cairo. For centuries, the tomb has been revered as a source of *baraka* (spiritual blessing): the sick travel here to be cured or to die at the mausoleum and, throughout history, the poor have settled around the tomb to seek the benevolence of visitors. This demonstrates how the phenomenon of people living in the cemeteries is not new. It is not only in the face of the twentieth century's housing crisis that people have settled among the dead. People have been living there for centuries (albeit for various reasons). Janet Abu-Lughod writes,

One should not imagine...that these cemeteries were (or are) used exclusively as burial sites. Although physically separated, they were never functionally segregated. From early times, among the shrines were found monasteries and schools for various religious and mystic orders. Some of these served as free hostels for itinerant scholars or travelers. In addition, guarding each family tomb was a resident retainer and his dependents. To this population must be added a few temporary and permanent squatters who found the rent-free stone and wooden structures of the 'tomb city' more spacious and substantial than the mud brick huts available to them within the city proper. With such a resident population, it was perhaps inevitable that some artisans and shopkeepers should gravitate to the area to fulfill the demand for daily goods and services. Nor were these the only functions of this unique land use. Just as the marshlands provided open recreational space for the militaristic sports pursued by the Mamlukes, the Cities of the Dead provided recreational facilities for the bulk of the population who repaired there weekly and, in even greater numbers, on the major festivals occasions. [20]

In this way, 'life' in the City of the Dead is as old as the City of the Dead itself.

Description

Recently, the Imam al-Shafi'i complex received a new arched entryway, parking area and sidewalks in front of the mosque.

Before stepping inside the mausoleum, stand back and appreciate the outside of the structure. The mausoleum is topped with a large bronze dome that can be seen from afar. The dome rises above the urban area that has been built up around the tomb over the years. Dating to A.D. 1722, the dome was the work of 'Ali Bey el-Kebir. It is made of two wooden shells, thirty centimeters apart. These shells

---

20   Abu-Lughod, Janet, <u>Cairo: 1001 Years of the City Victorious</u>, p.63.

are covered with lead and appear to be modeled after the Dome of the Rock in Jerusalem. At the dome's crest is a metal boat designed to hold grain for birds. The boat is also a Pharaonic symbol that represents the vessel that carries the dead to the afterworld.

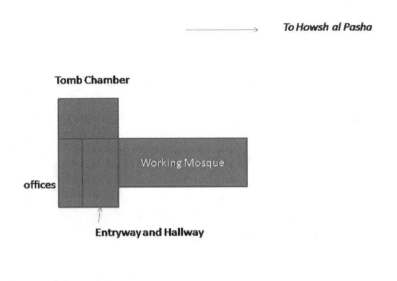

Layout of al-Shafi'i Mosque/Mausoleum

Walk down the long corridor into the entry hall. Here, there are offices on your left. Immediately in front of you, however, is a large, wooden door with metalwork decoration. This marks the entrance to the tomb chamber. Once inside, appreciate the beautiful painting on the walls at the base of the dome. The dome sits on stalactite squinches that are painted red and blue with gilt designs. The walls of the room are decorated with variegated marble that dates to the restoration of the building in the 1480s by the Mamluke Sultan Qaytbay (See Itinerary IV). The Imam's cenotaph is in the center of the room. Made of teak wood imported from India, it was hand carved by Ubayd ibn Ma'ali in A.D. 1178. It is considered to be one of the finest remaining examples of Ayyubid carving in wood. Surrounding the cenotaph is a lattice screen made of sandalwood that dates to A.D. 1911. The cenotaph is lit with green lights (green is the color of Islam and indicates life) and pilgrims will walk around it saying prayers and dropping pieces of paper through the lattice work with special requests and intentions written on them. At the back of the screen is a phallic-looking stela that is inscribed with verses from the Qur'an. Pilgrims can often be seen rubbing this stone with their hands seeking *baraka*. The marble column of the cenotaph marks the spot of the Imam's head. The green bulb in the shape of a turban was added in A.D. 1892.

The remaining cenotaphs in the room belong to members of the al-Hakim family. These include the cenotaph for Sayyid Muhammad 'Abd al-Hakam, the Sultan al-Kamil Ayyub and his mother.

In the mausoleum there are two *mihrabs* (the prayer niche that indicates the direction of Mecca which Muslims face when praying). The earlier one was not correctly in line with the city of Mecca. The second one, in correct orientation, was a donation of the Mamluke Sultan Qaytbay (See Itinerary IV for Qaytbay's history).

Leave the mausoleum and walk back into the entry hall. On your left, there will be a set of stairs leading to another hallway. At the end of this hallway is the entrance to the mosque of the Imam al-Shafi'i. The mosque is large and airy. The original structure was built in A.D. 1190 but was largely restored and rebuilt in A.D. 1763. The ceiling is wooden and is nicely painted with geometric designs and flower motifs. It is supported by marble columns. The mosque boasts of an attractive wooden pulpit with inlaid mother-of-pearl decoration. On the walls, handsome blue and white tiles provide a hint of Turkish influence. There is a balcony at the back of the mosque where women are allowed to pray, as traditionally, women pray behind the men in mosques so that they are not a distraction for the men during their worshiping of God. The floor of the mosque is covered with elegant oriental carpets.

The Imam al-Shafi'i's mosque is a working mosque. Notice the strings laid out along the floor that indicate where worshipers are to line up to pray as well as the plastic holders for shoes.

Access to Visitors

The Imam al-Shafi'i's mausoleum is open to the general public. Some visitors have been told that the mosque, however, is restricted to Muslim worshipers. This author has been fortunate to be allowed to enter the mosque on numerous occasions. As it is a working mosque, however, avoid prayer times. There is no admission fee to this mosque/mausoleum but the care-taker will expect, and most likely ask for, a small tip.

HOWSH AL-PASHA

From al-Shafi'i's mosque and mausoleum, walk out the front entrance and turn to the right. Walk through the gateway and take your first right. Walk among the tomb-homes until you reach the main road that runs parallel to the road that al-Shafi'i's is on. This requires walking along windy dirt alleyways but it is well worth the trek. Turn to your right and you will see a multi-domed structure up ahead. This is Howsh al-Pasha, the family cemetery of Muhammad 'Ali.

History

Howsh al-Pasha is the cemetery of the family of Muhammad Ali. Ali, often referred to as the founder of modern Egypt, became the creator of a dynasty that would rule Egypt from the early 1800s through 1952. Born in 1769, Muhammad Ali was a young officer in an Albanian contingent of the Ottoman army when he arrived in Egypt. Ali rose through the ranks of power rapidly and was soon the leader of the Albanian forces fighting for the Ottomans. It was at this time, around 1801, that there was a power struggle for the governorship of Egypt. Ali curried favor with the *ulama*, the leading religious officials in Islamic Egypt as well as Egypt's merchants who became supporters of Ali's and asked him to become governor. Although there was resistance from both the sitting Ottoman governor as well as the Mamlukes, Muhammad Ali was eventually proclaimed governor in 1805. The Mamlukes continued to make problems for Governor Ali in the early years that he was in office.

In 1811, however, Ali invited the last remaining Mamlukes to a ceremony at the Citadel. As they entered, they were all ambushed and killed, ridding Muhammad Ali of their resistance.

Once Ali had secured and consolidated his rule, he set out to strengthen the economy and to expand the military. His reform programs aimed at creating a modern Egypt after the European model. One of his most radical reforms was the expropriation of land. By 1815, most of Egypt's agricultural land was now in the hands of the state, providing significant revenues. Ali also improved irrigation systems and introduced new crops to Egypt. This included long staple cotton for which Egypt is famous today. Muhammad Ali also pursued modern industrial production. In this arena, however, he was less successful as Egypt lacked both sources of power as well as seasoned managers.

Muhammad Ali, himself illiterate until the age of 47, was also deeply concerned about education. Realizing that a modern society depends on an educated populace, Ali began schools to educate doctors, engineers and other specialists.

Muhammad Ali also conducted many successful military engagements. Along with his son, Ibrahim Pasha, Ali conducted victorious military campaigns against the Wahhabis in Arabia. In 1820, his armies were sent to conquer the Sudan. Fighting for the Ottoman Sultan, he also had victories in Greece until the British, French and Russians combined forces against him in 1827. For fighting in Greece, he was promised the governorship of Syria by Sultan Mahmud II. When the Sultan refused to make good on his promise, Muhammad Ali invaded Syria and moved on to Asia Minor in 1839. In a compromise agreement to end his advancement, the Sultan agreed to make the governorship of Egypt hereditary in Muhammad Ali's family line.

Ali retired from office in 1848 after a dose of silver nitrate given to him by his doctors to cure dysentery caused massive brain damage and resulted in bouts of madness. The reigns of the governorship were turned over to his son, Ibrahim who died a few months later and was replaced by Abbas, Ali's grandson.

Muhammad Ali died in Alexandria in 1849.

Description

This tomb complex encompasses the family cemetery of Muhammad Ali. Inside this complex are three of Ali's sons – Tusun, Ismail and Ibrahim – by his favorite wife Amina. In addition, there are the tombs of their wives and children, servants and other statesman and counselors. Ali had intended to be buried in this mausoleum but was instead buried in the Citadel.

Entrance to Howsh al Pasha

The seven unequal domes of Howsh al-Pasha are visible from the street behind the Imam al-Shafi-i's mausoleum. This is an unusual building that does not fit with traditional Ottoman architecture or any other traditional architectural style found in Cairo. It is suspected that Ali may have modified an existing mausoleum. The complex was (re)built in stages and may have originally only included five tomb chambers and no domes. The structure was remodeled and adapted to the needs of the family and the level of status they attained.

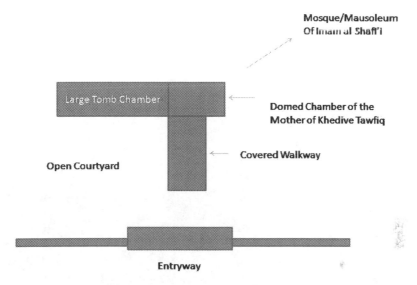

Layout of Howsh al-Pasha

Enter through the portal and you will find yourself in a barren *howsh* (courtyard). Visitors can close their eyes and imagine the rich green gardens that once filled this courtyard. From the courtyard, you can also admire the domes of the complex. The onion shape of these domes along with the ribbing and the small ribbed cap on the tops of the domes are an unprecedented combination in Islamic architecture in Egypt.

Follow the covered walkway into the tomb chambers. The first memorial, in a room of its own, is the domed chamber for the mother of Khedive Tawfiq. Tawfiq ruled Egypt from 1879 – 1892. The tomb is large, made of white marble and dates to 1884. Turn to the left and you will find a tomb surrounded by an immense bronze grill. This is the tomb of Tusun who died of the plague while on a military campaign in 1816. Immediately in front of Tusun lies Ismail who died in 1822 and was buried in the chamber that was originally intended for Muhammad Ali himself. It is believed that, after the death of two of Ali's sons, the domes were added to the complex. Two chambers away from Ismail's tomb is a tall cenotaph marking the burial place of Ibrahim Pasha. Under the adjoining dome are the cenotaphs of Abbas I, his son Ilhami Pasha, his wife, and Ahmed Rifat, the son of Ibrahim Pasha. King

Faruq, the last ruler from the Muhammad Ali family (1920 – 1965) lies in the white marble tomb. Also buried in this complex, several to a cenotaph, are the Mamlukes of Muhammad Ali.

The Domes of Howsh al Pasha

All of the cenotaphs are ornately carved and decorated with flowers and garlands and are brightly painted and gilded. Each cenotaph has a stela at the head that is topped with a head covering or with hair that demonstrates the rank and sex of the deceased. This gives visitors the feeling that they are walking among actual people who have been frozen in stone. Men are identified by such head coverings as fezzes or turbans. For women, coronets top the stela along with hair in various styles: braids denote a royal mother; painted braids a royal wife and; loose hair denotes a virgin princess.

Access to Visitors

Howsh al-Pasha is open to the public. There is a care-taker who will meet you when you enter the tomb complex. Tickets must be purchased to enter. At last check, an entry ticket was LE 10. An additional ticket was required in order to take pictures. The cost of this ticket was also LE 10.

CHAPTER 4

Itinerary III: The Basateen Cemetery

Featured Monuments:

- *Mosque of Sheikh Dandrawi*
- *Mausoleum of Abdel Halim al Hafez*
- *Mausoleum of Umm Kulthum*
- *Mauseoleum of Farid Atrash*

Estimated Time: 2 Hours

How to Get There: The Basateen Cemetery is at the end of the Southern Cemetery past the area surrounding the Mausoleum and Mosque of the Imam al Shafi'i. The easiest way to access this cemetery is from the Autostrade Highway. Driving south from the Citadel you will pass over the bridge that looks down over the al Shafi'i area of the Southern Cemetery. Immediately after the bridge and on your right is the beginning of an enormous government slaughterhouse. From the top of the bridge, one can see hundreds of cattle kept in pens. Stay along side the slaughterhouse walls until you find a street on your right. Turn into the cemetery from here. At the end of this street, you will join a perpendicular street. Off to your left you will see a colorful mosque with a minaret. This is the Mosque of Sheikh Dandrawi and the starting point for this itinerary.

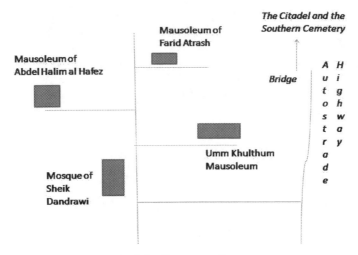

Map of the Basateen Cemetery

INTRODUCTION

Unlike the tombs described in this book located in the Cemetery of the Great, the Southern Cemetery and the Northern Cemetery, the tombs of the Basateen Cemetery represent a more modern face of Egypt. The Basateen Cemetery is a more contemporary extension of the Southern Cemetery. The tombs in this itinerary include a revered sheikh that lived until the mid-twentieth century and continues to have a large following among present-day Egyptians as well as three twentieth century Egyptian entertainers. Whereas the monuments that you will visit on this tour bear no special qualities architecturally, this itinerary provides the visitor with a look at the more modern face of the City of the Dead as well as a brief journey into Egyptian pop culture.

THE MOSQUE OF SHEIKH DANDRAWI

History

The man who would become known as Sheikh Dandrawi was born in Dendera in Upper Egypt. He is said to have been a very pious man who devoted his life to prayer and to helping others in need of spiritual direction. He was given the title of Sufi[21] sheikh and soon developed a large group of followers -- a group which still exists and is expanding today, decades after his death in 1951. Every year, hundreds of followers, mostly from Upper Egypt, come to Sheikh Dandrawi's mosque and mausoleum to celebrate his moulid or religious festival. The moulid is held on the anniversary of his death (26 Gamad Second 1372, Islamic Calendar) as Sheikh Dandrawi's birthday is not known. The moulid brings these pilgrims together for a combination of prayer, religious instruction, and celebration and is mostly financed by one of Dandrawi's living sons.

Description

The Dandrawi complex consists of two long buildings sitting parallel to each other and separated by a covered courtyard. The buildings are most easily approached from the south. As you enter the courtyard, to the left are offices and rooms for washing in preparation for prayer. To the right is the mosque and mausoleum. The rooms of this complex are modern and lack any outstanding decoration or architectural style. Still, Dandrawi is worth a visit as an example of a modern, functional mosque and mausoleum and allows visitors to witness the devotion of Sheikh Dandrawi's followers (as there is usually a constant flow of activity at the mosque).

The mosque and the tomb area are made of brick covered by cement and are painted light green with geometric designs gracing the bottom half of the walls. Florescent lights and white ceiling fans as well as plastic chandeliers reassure the visitor that the house of God comes in many shapes and sizes. One unique aspect of the mosque is the mihrab. This prayer niche is kitty-cornered at the south-east end of the long room – the first time that I have seen this phenomenon in Cairo. There is also an impressive wooden pulpit.

The tomb area follows the mosque and is marked by a large wooden door bearing a silver medallion. The room has a simple painted dome over the

---

21 A Sufi is a member of an Islamic religious group which tries to achieve
    unity with God by living a simple life and by praying and meditating.

cenotaph, which is covered with velvet and bears silver plates and banisters. The cenotaph itself is enclosed in a small room made of mashrabeya and covered by a small dome. The door to this room is blanketed in silver. The room is lit by green lights (green is the color of Islam) and a chandelier. Arabic sayings grace the walls of the room and there are typically dried flower decorations that have been left by pilgrims.

Access to Visitors

Although Sheikh Dandrawi is a modern, functioning mosque, non-Muslims have been allowed to enter the mosque and mausoleum. Still, my experience has shown that the Dandrawi followers have become increasingly suspicious of visitors in recent times. The followers of Sheikh Dandrawi are traditionally Sufi but would like to be recognized as a separate and autonomous group. They feel that their group is large and has found the straight path of Islam. They seek to be directly under God and the Prophet and not under an umbrella organization. The Egyptian government, Al-Azhar[22], and other Sufis have opposed this separation. Due to this conflict, outsiders are frequently viewed with suspicion as – one follower explained to me - the Dandrawis feel that the government may attempt to infiltrate the group to follow their activities.

THE MAUSOLEUM OF ABDEL HALIM AL HAFEZ

Leave the Mosque and Mausoleum of Sheikh Dandrawi and drive north a short way on the main street. Take the very first left north of Sheikh Dandrawi. About 500 feet down this street on the right is a colorful tomb which is the resting place of Abdel Halim al Hafez.

History

Abdel Halim al Hafez is without a doubt one of the most famous (if not *the* most famous) actor/singer in Egypt's modern history. Posters of him still grace the walls of young Egyptians' bedrooms and hardly a day

---

22 Al-Azhar is the oldest and most respected university in Egypt and issues judgments on religious issues.

goes by when one of his black and white films is not showing on one of Egypt's television channels.

Born in 1929 in the small Delta village of Helwat, Abdel Halim faced difficulty early with the death of his mother shortly after his birth and the later death of his father. Still, his extraordinary musical talent was recognized as early as primary school and he went on to graduate from Cairo's Institute of Arabic Music and the Higher Institute for Theater Music with a specialization as an oboe player. Shortly after his graduation, the famous Egyptian singer Karem Mahmoud was set to sing live on national radio and was unable to make the performance. Halim, an unknown on the national scene, was chosen as a substitute and was thrust into the limelight when Hafez Abdel Al Wahab, the head of the musical programs on national radio was listening and became determined to make Abdel Halim a star. Indeed, Halim would become known as the "nightingale" of Arabic music.

In 1954, Halim sang at the anniversary of the Egyptian Revolution. He would become known for his patriotic songs of Arab nationalism such as "Sora" (Picture) and "Al Sad al A'li (The High Dam) that appealed to the hopes and dreams of Arabs. The words and rhythm of his songs were kept simple, making them easy for people to remember and identify with.

Abdel Halim was also noted for his touching love songs, inspired by his own difficulties in love. His love for a young girl whose parents refused to let him marry her and who later died from disease has a strong influence on his art.

In addition to his music, Abdel Halim became a favorite of the Egyptian silver screen, appearing in fourteen movies between 1955 and 1969.

Abdel Halim had contracted bilharzia as a child and the disease eventually led to his death in 1977. His death brought about a national mourning to Egypt as the country had lost its most talented, inspirational, and patriotic star.

Description

Abdel Halim's tomb is colorful both inside and outside reflecting the entertainer's personality and the joy that he brought to Egyptians during his lifetime. Made of brick, the tomb is painted bright red and well-kept by a full-time guard. The tomb is an open-air courtyard with a raised portion at the back where the remains of Abdel Helim and his brother are interred. The rest of Abdel Halim's family is buried in a chamber under the courtyard. A marble slab in the floor with protruding metal handles covers the entrance to that chamber.

Abdel Halim's Tomb

The back portion of the tomb is covered and separated from the courtyard by three arches. Under the middle arch is a picture of Abdel Halim with an Egyptian flag hung behind it. To the right is the white granite cenotaph marking Abdel Halim's burial plot. The black calligraphic inscriptions are verses from the Qur'an.

On the right side of the tomb's entrance is a bathroom and a small room for the caretaker. To the left is the high-light of the visit to Abdel Halim's tomb -- a mosaic of pictures of Abdel Halim that shows him throughout his life. Bordering the mosaic of photographs is an Egyptian flag. The decor of his tomb clearly reflects the personality that made Abdel Halim famous as a young, patriotic, pop idol.

Access to Visitors

On any clear day in Cairo, one is likely to find visitors at Abdel Halim's tomb. If the tomb is locked, ask the local children for Hagg Ahmed Saber, the tomb's care-keeper who lives two tombs down and across the street. The tomb is especially crowded every March 30th, the anniversary of Abdel Halim's death. To mark the anniversary, living family members come to the tomb from their homes in the Delta and spend the day playing a combination of Qur'anic music as well as music from Abdel Halim's records and films. Security is often needed to keep visitors at bay.

Foreign visitors to the tomb will often be surrounded by local children asking for money.

THE MAUSOLEUM OF UMM KULTHUM

Return to the main street from Abdel Halim's tomb and turn right. Drive slowly and after a few thousand feet you will see a large tomb on your right. Turn down the small street following the tomb. Drive a short way and on your left will be a cement wall with the branches of trees spilling over into the street. This is the tomb of Umm Kulthum.

History

Umm Kulthum was born to a poor family in a small rural village in the Nile Delta region of Egypt. Her exact date of birth is not known for certain but is thought to be May 4, 1904. Her father, Sheikh Ibrahim al-Sayyid al-Baltaji was the *imam* (the man who leads prayer in a mosque) of the local mosque who moonlighted as a singer at weddings and other celebrations in order to supplement the family income.

At the age of five, Umm Kulthum was enrolled in a Qur'anic school where she learned the basic skills of reading and writing and memorized sections of the Qu'ran. She learned to sing from her father and began performing in her village at a young age. Given her strong voice and youth, she became popular among the villagers and was soon the primary draw for her father's singing group. As she became increasingly well-liked, the group began to travel to more distant villages to perform and, eventually, considered taking Umm Kulthum to the center of Egypt's music industry -- Cairo.

In 1923, after her father had made initial contacts in the industry, the move to Cairo was finally accomplished. Umm Kulthum's voice was immediately noticed by the local media but was considered to be unschooled. As a result, her father hired several music teachers to work with her and refine her talents. At the same time, Umm Kulthum polished her personal behaviors and appearance to emulate the elite of Cairene society.

Part of the process of refining and modernizing her music and appearance involved replacing family members as her back-up with professional and accomplished musicians. In addition, she broadened her musical repertoire from traditional religious songs to more modern love songs, many of which were written specifically for her. With these improvements, Umm Kulthum catapulted to the top of Egypt's music industry. From her first commercial recordings in the 1920s, Kulthum branched out into radio, film and television.

In the 1940s, she took a departure from modern love songs and promoted songs with an indigenous Egyptian style. These songs were well received by the populous and resulted in a decade that is known as the "Golden Age" of Umm Kulthum.

Unfortunately, Umm Kulthum was hindered by health problems beginning in the 1930s. These included problems with her thyroid, liver and gall bladder. A period of improved health allowed her to resume a more normal schedule in the mid-1950s when she began to collaborate with the popular composer Muhammad abd al-Wahab to create new, modern love songs that appealed to younger Egyptians. During the following decade and a half, Umm Kulthum participated more in Egyptian public life and advocated many causes, including strong Egyptian nationalism following Egypt's defeat in the 1967 War. Kulthum performed many concerts internationally and within Egypt and gave the proceeds of these performances to the government of Egypt to help strengthen the state.

Beginning in 1971, Umm Kulthum's health began to seriously decline and she sought treatment in Europe and the United States. On February 3, 1975, she suffered a heart attack and died. Her funeral was postponed for two days to accommodate the great number of mourners who were traveling from other countries to pay their respects. Still, organizers were not prepared for the millions of mourners who turned out and her body was carried for more than three hours through the streets of Cairo before being brought to its burial place in the Basateen Cemetery.

Description

Umm Kulthum's grand tomb dwarfs all others in the surrounding area with its height, large courtyard and intimidating wall. The entrance to the courtyard is through two large metal doors. The cement face of the tomb is regal with a high doorway and an impressive, large wooden door. When you step inside, you cannot help but feel that you are *not* in a tomb. Rather, it is as if you have stepped into the living room of a palace from Egypt's glory days. The room is large and airy. In the center of the room is a sofa and chairs in the so-called *"Louis-Farouk"* style as well as end tables, a coffee table, carpets and arrangements of plastic flowers. Chandeliers hang from the ceiling.

The floor is covered with beige ceramic tiles of the kind found in many modern Egyptian homes.

The Interior of Umm Kulthum's Mausoleum

To understand that this room is actually a mausoleum, you have to look at the four corners where slabs of gray marble mark the burial spots of Umm Kulthum and members of her family (there are no formal gravestones). Umm Kulthum's body lies under the floor on the front right side of the room. Her mother is at the back right side and her brother is buried to the front left side of the room. An empty tomb chamber is at the back left side. Be careful not to step on the marble slabs as it would be considered a sign of disrespect.

At the back of the room to the left there is a small table with a guest book where visitors can sign their names and leave any thoughts and wishes for Umm Kulthum. Browsing through the guest book is a delight as there are passages written in many different languages, especially French, demonstrating Umm Kulthum's international popularity.

Another peculiar feature of this tomb is a frame with calligraphy hanging on the wall behind the sofa. Depending on which direction you view the frame from, the writing says something different – all referring to Umm Kulthum. If looked at from directly in front, the writing reads her name; from the right side, it reads *"kowcap Sharik"* or "Star of the Middle East"; from the left side, it reads *"Sitt al Khoal"* or "Lady of Everyone" – an Arabic term of respect for women.

One leaves this mausoleum with two impressions: First, the tomb makes it easier to understand how people can live in the cemeteries given its home-like qualities. Certainly, not all of the tombs of the City of the Dead have the infrastructure and facilities as Umm Kulthum's. Nonetheless, one gets a feel for how a tomb can be made into a home. Secondly, as with the mausoleum of Abdel Halim al Hafez, the tomb of Umm Kulthum reflects her personality which made her beloved to Egyptians. The tomb is clean and simple, yet elegant. It is a reminder of the classy and sophisticated woman of humble roots that Umm Kulthum was.

Access to Visitors

The tomb is kept locked. One of the neighbors living in the tomb on the right-side corner at the beginning of the street has the key. Ask a local child to fetch it for you. The care-keeper will expect a small tip for opening the tomb.

THE MAUSOLEUM OF FARID ATRASH

From Umm Kulthum's tomb, return to the main street and continue north. After two curves in the street, you will find a fairly large, dirt street on your right. If you look down the street you can see a bridge of the Autostrade Highway in the distance. Turn left here. Farid Atrash's tomb is the second on the left.

History

Farid Al-Atrash was born at the beginning of the twentieth century in the area of Mount Druze, then a Syrian province in the Ottoman Empire. Al-Atrash's family was wealthy and his father was the leader of the Druze community. Al-Atrash's family led a rebellion against the French in the region after World War I. With the family in danger due to their role in the rebellion, al-Atrash's mother Princess Alia took her children and fled to Egypt leaving her husband and the family wealth behind. The princess disguised herself and children by taking on a fake name upon arrival in Cairo.

Growing up in Old Cairo, Farid played the *oud* (lute) and managed to get a contract with a local band. By 1934, some of his *oud* solo recordings were being played by the Egyptian Broadcasting Authority.

Young Farid attended the French school in Cairo which waived the tuition for the child. During his school years, he began to become increasingly interested in music and was allowed to train with the school's Christian choir. According to Sami Asmar, his instructor was not immediately impressed with Farid's talent as he had a nice voice but seemed unable to express his feelings. The instructor "advised him to cry so that the listeners would feel the pain expressed in the chants. As his fans know, this advice worked, and remained a theme that lasted throughout his career, and clearly earned him the label of 'sad singer'". [23]

Still, Farid Al-Atrash did not become an overnight sensation. Rather, his sister Esmahan became a more famous singer and helped her brother by getting him a part in her first film production, *Intisar Al Shebab* (The Victory of Youth). Esmahan died in a drowning

---

23　Asmar, Sami, "Remembering Farid al-Atrash: A Contender in the Age of Giants", Al Jadid, Vol. 4, No. 22, 1998.

accident, however, in 1944. Following his sister's death, Farid would go on to become one of the most famous singers/actors in Egypt.

Faird Al-Atrash would end up recording more than 500 songs and appeared in 31 films. Atrash was a favorite of the Egyptian public who saw him as a symbol of romance. He competed fiercely with Abdel Halim al Hafez for popularity. Still, Farid always felt that he was shunned by the Egyptian music industry that viewed him as a foreigner. He was deeply disappointed that Umm Kulthum refused to sing any of his songs and Egyptian critics tended to be very harsh on Atrash. In 1970, President Gamal Abdel Nasser gave Atrash the Badge of Merit, first class. Still, Atrash was said to be dissatisfied that he did not receive the more prestigious Medal of Honor as was given to Umm Kulthum.

Atrash faired just as poorly in love and never married. Some accounts say that one of Farid's failed love interests involved Egyptian royalty. According to one account,

"Shortly before the Egyptian revolution, Farid befriended the king's wife. The playboy king was uncomfortable sharing the spotlight with another celebrity but soon found himself forced out of the country. After getting a divorce from the exiled king, the wife returned to Egypt where a stormy love affair with al-Atrash was the buzz of the tabloids. Her family, however, rejected Farid for their daughter, partly due to political reasons in the revolutionary environment of the nation. This loss led Farid into [a] long period of depression not unfamiliar to the sad singer, and started health problems that worsened from then until his death." [24]

He died in Beirut in December 1974 at the approximate age of sixty. At the funeral procession, thousands of fans walked behind his coffin.

---

24 Asmar, Sami, "Remembering Farid al-Atrash: A Contender in the Age of Giants", Al Jahdid, Vol. 4, No. 22, 1998.

Description

Farid Attash's tomb is rather simple and not as well kept when compared to Abdel Halim al Hafez's or Umm Kulthum's mausoleums. The tomb is a fairly small cement structure with a tall door that is kitty-cornered at the south-east end of the tomb. The tall metal door is blemished by graffiti. Inside is a plain room with two cenotaphs on a raised area at the back of the room. The cenotaphs are made of white marble and bear numerous verses of Islamic calligraphy in black inscription. The cenotaphs are for Farid and his sister. There are also two small benches of white marble for visitors to sit and pray or to reflect on Farid's life and accomplishments. Above the cenotaphs are two pictures of Farid Attash – one a photograph and the other done in needlework.

Access to Visitors

Farid Attash's tomb is no longer as popular a place of visitation as Abdel Halim al Hafez's or Umm Kulthum's. Still, access is easy. Simply ask one of the locals lingering in the street for the key and it will undoubtedly appear. In the past, there has been a woman with an amputated leg that sits in front of a tomb a short distance from Farid Attash's mausoleum. She appears to be the care-taker and will ask visitors for LE 10 in backsheesh. A smaller tip is acceptable.

CHAPTER 5
Itinerary IV: The Northern Cemetery

Featured Monuments:

- *The Tomb of Qansuh Abu*
- *Sa'id*
- *The Complex of Sultan Inal*
- *The Complex of the Amir*
- *Qurqumus*
- *The War (Martyr's) Cemetery*
- *The Complex of Farag ibn*
- *Barquq*
- *The Complex of Sultan Barsbay*
- *The Complex of Sultan Qaytbay*
- *The Tomb of Princess Tughay*

Estimated Time: 2 Hours and 30 Minutes

How to get there: The Northern Cemetery is wedged in between Salah Salem Highway and the Autostrade Highway. It runs lengthwise from the northern edge of the Citadel to the outskirts of Nasr City. This tour will begin at the northern tip of the cemetery. Follow Salah Salem Highway north from the Citadel along side the cemetery. Pass under a foot bridge and continue straight until you reach a bridge that passes over a crossing street. Do not take the bridge. Instead, turn right under the bridge and enter the Northern Cemetery. Take your first left and in front of you will be an elongated monument in the center of a modern street. This is the Tomb of Qansun Ab Sa'id and is the start of itinerary IV.

INTRODUCTION

The area that would become known as the Northern Cemetery was largely uninhabited desert before the Mamluke era (A.D. 1250 – A.D. 1517). Mamluke rule is typically divided into two separate periods: the Bahris and the Circassians. Mamlukes were originally brought to Egypt as slaves and were trained in Arabic, Islam and military techniques as well as discipline. They became Egypt's main military battle force under the Ayyubids. The Mamlukes, however, seized power from their rulers and set up their own dynasty that would last for more than 250 years. The Bahri Mamlukes were Turks from the region north of the Caspian Sea. The Circassian Mamlukes, who ruled from 1382 - 1517, were from the region between the Black Sea and the Caspian Sea.

After seizing power in A.D. 1250, the Mamlukes built their hippodrome in the area of the Northern Cemetery. Shortly thereafter, the area also became the base for Sufi mystics. These holy men chose to live outside of the city in isolation in order to devote themselves to prayer and spiritual contemplation. The Sufi sheikhs were buried in this area and their tombs became popular sites for Islamic pilgrims. Mamluke rulers - who had made Sufism a state institution - built khanqahs, or monasteries, for these Sufis in the Northern Cemetery. These complexes would contain the tomb of the leader who had financed their construction. Mamlukes believed that such veneration to the Sufis and the placement of their tombs among the Sufis would benefit them in the afterlife. They would also contain mosques, madrasas, travelers' quarters, mills, bakeries and other facilities.

These mosques and monasteries continued to be mainly surrounded by desert through the end of the Mamluke reign. Under the Ottomans and in subsequent centuries, however, more modern tombs - which pale in comparison to the architectural achievements of the Mamlukes - have filled in the vacancies between the major tombs. The Northern Cemetery is sometimes referred to as the 'Tombs of the Caliphs'. This is false, however, as the Tomb of the Abbasid Caliphs is located in the

Cemetery of the Great (See Itinerary I). The Northern Cemetery is sometimes referred to as the Eastern Cemetery as well.

Today, the Northern Cemetery is one of the most urbanized areas of the City of the Dead. In between the monuments described in this Chapter, you will find a thriving Cairo neighborhood with paved roads, stores, cafes, apartment buildings and a police station.

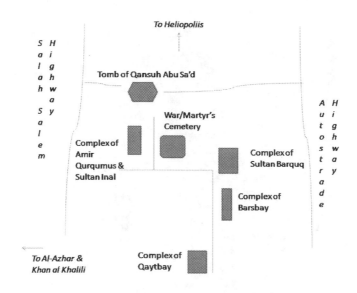

Map of the Northern Cemetery

THE TOMB OF QANSUH ABU SA'ID

History

Qansuh Abu Sa'id was purchased by the Sultan Qaytbay when he was a young Circassian boy. Soon, however, it was discovered that Qansuh was the brother of the favorite concubine of Qaytbay. As a result, he was given the position of Dawadar[25]. Qansuh became sultan for a period of a little over one year (1498 – 1500) but was deposed and exiled to Alexandria.

---

25   A Dawadar is an amir from among the men who share in the group feeling of the ruler. The ruler usually relies upon him, trusts him, and confides in him.

Description

Tomb Monument of Qansuh Abu Sa'id

This tomb chamber was built in 1499 and was originally part of a larger complex. All that remains now stands in the middle of a major road that connects Salah Salem Highway with the Autostrade Highway. The fact that the road provides open space around the tomb allows the visitor to appreciate the building without the distraction of adjoining buildings. The impressive structure stands tall with its square base topped by a dome with interesting carved decorations and an unusual support. The dome is carved with star rosettes surrounded by a triple arrow design. This is a variation from the typical arabesques that dominated surface decoration during this period. The other unusual feature is found in the pediment (triangular units) used in the exterior design of the dome support, forming three tiers of half-pyramids.

Access to Visitors

This tomb is not accessible to the general public but it is worth admiring the structure and the unique features of the dome and the dome support from the safety of the side of the road. Be careful as the monument is located in the middle of a busy Cairo street.

THE COMPLEX OF SULTAN INAL & THE COMPLEX OF THE AMIR QURQUMUS

From the Tomb of Qansun Ab Sa'id, look southward (towards the Citadel) and you will see a large Mamluke complex surrounded by a wrought iron fence. At first glance, this complex appears to be one entity. At closer inspection, however, the eye can discern that it is actually two separate complexes built beside each other: that of the Sultan Inal and that of the Amir Qurqumas. Go to the most southern point of the complex to enter. If there is no one visibly at the complex, go to the coffee shop across the street to the south and ask about the care-taker.

Given that these two complexes are adjoining, I am putting them together for the purposes of this itinerary but will discuss the history and description of the two complexes separately below. Although you will come to Inal's complex first upon arrival, I will present the complex of Amir Qurqumus before Inal's as the most common entrance to these complexes is to the south, making it more logical for a visitor to initially enter Qurqumus' complex.

Jeffrey A. Nedoroscik

THE COMPLEX OF THE AMIR QURQUMUS

Complex of Amir Qurqumus

History

Qurqumus was a Mamluke of the Sultan Qaytbay. Qurqumus was said to become an excellent military officer, rising through the ranks from 'Second Equerry' to 'Commander of 1,000'. He was named the Governor of Aleppo but was never actually able to take up the post because he was imprisoned in the citadel in Damascus by the Sultan of Syria, Amir Tumanbay. When Qansuh al-Ghuri came to power in Egypt, he was released and returned to Cairo. Under Sultan al-Ghuri, he became the Grand Amir or *Amir Kabir* -- the Commander-in-Chief of the armies. Qurqumus was said to be vehemently anti-Ottoman and died in 1510, just a few years before the Ottomans overthrew the Mamlukes and took power in Egypt. Qurqumus was known as a man of great integrity and modesty. His death sent all of Cairo into mourning.

The following is a historical obituary and account of Qurqumus' funeral:

> The death of Qurqumus the Atabaki, Grand Marshall of the Armies of Egypt, occurred on Tuesday the 23rd (of Ramadan). Cairo went into mourning and his funeral procession was followed by a numerous throng. The four Qadis (judges) were there, and all the officers, junior and senior, the principal civil officials and the notables. One could say that no one of importance was missing in the funeral cortege. Penitential alms of bread, dates and sheep were carried before it, but when it arrived at the college of Sultan Hasan, the common people seized these. At various points along the route, pieces of silver (money) were thrown over the bier. Sorrow and weeping were general because Qurqumus was both benevolent and modest. When the procession arrived at the Sabil of al-Mu'mini, the Sultan (Ghuri) left the Hippodrome and came on horse to the fountain. He dismounted and entered the oratory. When they placed the bier in front of him, the Sultan kissed the dead man, and then wept bitterly. After the prayer, the Sultan helped carry the coffin for some paces, then the officers took over in relays as they passed in front of the procession. They went to the mausoleum built by the deceased in the desert next to that of al-Ashraf Inal. He was buried under the dome, God have mercy on him.[26]

Description

Qurqumas built this mausoleum before his death in 1510. In addition to the mausoleum, the complex contained numerous buildings including a *rab'* (apartment building), which was used to accommodate travelers and to provide monetary support for the complex's operating costs. It

---

26   This account is attributed to Ibn Iyas and was found on the touregypt.net webpage in an article by Ismail Abaxa entitled "The Funerary Complex of Amir Qurqumus".

also contained a madrasa-mosque, residential quarters, a sabil-kuttab as well as kitchens, storerooms, stables, waterwheels, and an ablution court.

During the British occupation of Egypt, this structure was used as a storeroom for gunpowder. In more modern times, the complex has been undergoing extensive restoration by the Polish-Egyptian Group for Restoration of Islamic Monuments.

You will enter the compound through the southern gate. The complex of Qurqumus will be in front of you with the arcades of the reception area appearing to your right. Most of the arches of these arcades have been restored and are impressive. Notice the wooden doors that line the main building. Many of these have six-pointed stars carved above the doorways. Stars were seen as a guiding force and a natural part of the decoration of religious buildings.

The care-taker will want to bring you into the buildings from a back entrance. Instead, walk around the front of the building to the northern side and enter through the main portal. Notice the ablaq masonry of the façade. As you enter through the main door, the sabil-kuttab will be on your left. This room held the water dispensary and is where the washing of the hands, face and feet took place prior to entering the mosque. One floor above the sabil is the kuttab or qur'anic school. To the right of the doorway is the minaret. Proceed up the steps to your right and enter the mosque-madrasa. This room is an open courtyard that has been partially restored. Notice the wood around the doorways with star and other geometric patterns. Also, there are impressive marble panels covering the lower halves of the walls. At the back of the room, there is a beautiful balcony made of wooden mashrabiya. One can get a closer look at the balcony by climbing up the stairs located down a passageway on the north side of the room close to where you entered. When you reach the balcony, look closely at the wooden ceiling above. Part of the ceiling has been poorly restored but part is original. The original ceiling is decorated with intricate carved designs and Islamic calligraphy. These patterns were once a ray of color and traces of the original red color can still be seen in places.

Return to the stairs and advance to the second floor. At the front of the building is a nice balcony that looks out over the main street. The mashrabiya wood of this balcony is not original but a more contemporary copy. The inscription '1415' was on the original and is repeated on the copy. The other rooms on this floor were cells for Sufis and are usually kept locked. As you return to the stairs, notice how the sunlight brilliantly shines through the mashrabiya windows at the end of the narrow hallway.

Climb to the roof for a close inspection of the dome and minaret as well as a complete view of the entire compound. The roof is lined with slabs of masonry in the shape of open flower buds. This type of cresting was typical of the middle Mamluke period. The dome and the minaret are intricately carved. The exterior of the dome is decorated with carved lozenges (a four-sided planar figure with a diamond-like shape) at the bottom that abruptly give way to a zigzag pattern that rises to the tip of the dome. The pattern is repeated on the minaret. The bent supports that can be seen on the minaret were once used for hanging lamps. The minaret is divided into three sections: the first with 5 small balconies; the second with one large balcony that encircles the minaret's core; the third is open and also has one large, circular balcony.

Return to the mosque-madrasa and continue to the rest of the complex by entering through a doorway at the south-east corner of the room. This is the tomb chamber with its tall dome. Members of the family of the Amir Qurqumus are buried under your feet. Upon close inspection of the floor tiles, you can discern which tiles are removed to gain access to the burial chamber below. Qurqumus himself is buried in the adjoining room. [27]

On the south side of the tomb chamber is the qasr, which literally translates as "palace". This was a residence and can be entered from the back of the complex (where the care-taker would normally first take visitors) or from an internal staircase on the south side of the tomb chamber. In Mamluke times, it was the custom for wealthy people to include such residential buildings (as you will see in the following

---

[27] In recent times, this room has been used as the workshop for the restoration workers.

descriptions of the complexes of Inal, Barquq, Barsbay and Qaytbay). Some of these residential units were built to accommodate Sufi sheiks. Others were used by the families for visitation on feast days and holidays – a practice that is continued in modern times in Egypt.

The building has large windows with iron grills that are topped with arches. The rooms on the ground level were used for storage and stables. The first floor includes an open courtyard, a reception area, a bedroom and a toilet. These rooms are rather plain. The wooden ceilings have been rebuilt and poorly restored and little of the original decoration is left.

Return to the door where you originally entered the mosque-madrasa. As you leave, notice the small room at the bottom of the stairs. This was the bath. In the middle of the room are the remains of a small water fountain. At the back of the room are two small cups projecting from the wall that served as toilets.

Behind the main complex existed a rab' or series of apartments, some of which still exist and have been restored. The small cells have vaulted ceilings and thin, elongated windows. Here, you will find apartments built on two floors with a toilet on each floor of the apartment. The apartments are made up of cells set along a corridor in four symmetrical pairs connected by a spiral staircase. They could each house up to eight people. Opposite these cells is an area that acted as storerooms and kitchens. Beyond that is a cemetery for Sufis.

COMPLEX OF SULTAN INAL

History

Inal was a Mamluke of the Sultan Barquq who rose through the ranks of the military and government to the ultimate position of Sultan. Inal began as the Amir Tablkhana or "Amir of Forty" and then became the Governor of Edessa in Syria. Later, he was the Chief Dawadar and then al-Amir al-Kabir (Commander-in-Chief of the Armies) before becoming Sultan in 1451. When Inal became Sultan, he was 73 years old and would rule over a thriving Egypt for 7 years.

Description

Sultan Inal's complex was built over the course of his career and its physical composition reflects the fact that he held many different positions and levels of authority throughout his career. Separate sections of his complex mark each era of his ascension to power.

Inal constructed his complex in the Northern Cemetery over the latter part of his career. The mausoleum was built when he was Amir. When he became Sultan, the khanqh, madrasa-mosque, a sabil, and a *zawiya* (a residence for Muslim Sufis centered around a sheikh) were added. As a result, the complex has an odd appearance. The dome, built early in the construction, sits low in proportion to the rest of the structure. Inal's complex represents the only building in Cairo that demonstrates the various ranks that a leader had achieved. Author/Historian William Lyster describes this demonstration of power and rank through the size and grandeur of buildings as part of a "cultural rivalry" that Mamlukes enjoyed. He writes;

> "The intense rivalry among the Mamluk *amirs* also found expression in the field of culture. Status in Mamluk society was dependent on extravagant displays of wealth. The splendor of an *amir's* lifestyle, the quality of his possessions and the grandeur of his building projects were as much symbols of his power as were his rank and position within the military hierarchy. The resulting cultural rivalry, in which each *amir* tried to outshine his fellow Mamluks, was responsible, in part, for the numerous funerary complexes that today grace the City of the Dead." [28]

The façade of Sultan Inal's mausoleum, like Qurqumus' complex, is ablaq masonry. The main portal is vaulted and impressive. To the left of the portal is the minaret which is detached, connected to the main structure only by a wall. To the right is the domed tomb chamber.

---

28   Lyster, William, "The City of the Dead", Cairo Today, March 1988, page 35.

Begin at the northern end of the complex at the domed mausoleum. Inside, the cenotaphs are in a state of disrepair. In general, Sultan Inal's complex is in significantly worse condition than Qurqumus' and badly in need of repair and restoration. The windows of the mausoleum are broken and the Islamic calligraphy is faded. Still, through the few hints of color and decoration that remain, one can capture the magic the room once possessed. To the left of the mausoleum was a sabil-kuttab but the second floor has been destroyed.

Leave the mausoleum and enter the mosque-madrasa by a small stairway to your left. The doorway is decorated with a *conch* (a recessed area in the shape of a conch shell) design on stalactites. The mosque-madrasa is airy and open and is built in a modified cruciform layout and was probably not built until around 1456. This mosque-madrasa is fairly small, a trend in the second half of the fifteenth century as cells for Sufis were moved out of the mosque-madrasa and into independent buildings. The middle area of this room was always uncovered. The east and west sections, however, were once covered by a wooden roof that is now completely missing. Also missing are the marble panels that once covered the walls. The prayer niche is of carved stone with a conch on top. There is a sunrise motif filling the conch.

From the outside, inspect the dome. It is made of stone with a zigzag carved pattern. One unusual feature is found at the base of the dome where there are circles of blue glass paste filling carved loops.

The unattached minaret has a stone shaft that is highly carved. Its base has decorative panels. The first story has keel-arched niches with colonnettes in between, carved with arabesques. Inscriptional bands decorate the upper levels of the minaret. The second story is also decorated with a zigzag pattern.

Access for Visitors

The complexes of Sultan Inal and the Amir Qurqumus were not officially open to the public at the time of the publication of this guide. The Egyptian Antiquities Organization, who supervises these monuments, has been working with a Polish group to restore these monuments since 1983 and hope to open these complexes as tourist venues in the future. At this time, however, one has to have a bit of luck to be allowed into the complexes. There is a care-taker named Ahmed at the Qurqumus complex who is entrusted with the key to both mosques and mausoleums and can be persuaded to give tours of the monuments. A small tip will be expected. Ask for Ahmed at the small coffee shop to the south of the monuments.

THE WAR (MARTYR'S) CEMETERY

History

Across the main street to the east of the complexes of Inal and Qurqumus is the War (Martyr's) Cemetery. It is walled and there is a large entryway with a plaque commemorating the cemetery, dedicated to the war dead of the 1967 and 1973 battles between Egypt and Israel. Here, lay the bodies of the soldiers that were unidentified and buried anonymously. The cemetery is maintained by the Egyptian military.

Description

As you walk in the gates you will feel that you have walked into a different world. This 'cemetery within a cemetery' is much more serene than the Northern Cemetery in general. Filled with greenery and flowers, the War Cemetery is generally kept quite clean by its care-takers.

There is a white entryway with black wrought iron gates. As you enter, immediately in front of you there will be a small courtyard with a column dedicated to the war dead. Branching out from this courtyard, white marble tombs form perfect rows. Each tomb is exactly the same, quietly pronouncing the anonymity of all of the soldiers buried here. The white marble tombs bear no writing. Rather, they are blank.

Following the rows of graves there is an elongated mosque. Additional graves lie behind the mosque.

Take time to walk between the tombs and even sit down for a few minutes to capture the atmosphere of tragedy, yet tranquility, that the environment provokes. The cemetery is both eerie and peaceful and seems to speak to all of the contrasting emotions that war brings forth.

Access for Visitors

Foreigners are allowed to enter the War Cemetery. There is no entrance fee but a tip to the care-takers will be expected. The cemetery is open daily between 8 AM and 4 PM.

One can also view the War Cemetery from the porch of the neighboring Mosque and Mausoleum of Sultan Barquq (See below).

THE COMPLEX OF FARAG IBN BARQUQ

Leave the entrance of the War Cemetery and continue south until you come to the end of the road. You now have the choice to turn left or right. Turn left and you will find a monumental Mamluke complex in front of you. This is the Mosque and Mausoleum of Farag Ibn Barquq and it is one of the major Mamluke complexes in the Northern Cemetery.

History

The first of the Burgi Mamlukes, Sultan Barquq ruled from 1382-99. His mortuary complex was built over the course of eleven years by his son Farag, who honored his request to be buried next to the tombs of revered Sufi sheikhs. The complex is built in massive Mamluke-style architecture and contains twin domes, twin minarets, as well as a pair of sabil-kuttabs.

Sultan Barquq was actually of Circassian origin and was recruited under the Bahri Mamlukes. Circassians were first brought to Egypt as slave troops in the thirteenth century under the rule of Sultan Qalawun. Freed in 1363, Barquq seized power in 1382 following a series of plots and assassinations and began the era of the Circassian Mamlukes, also referred to as the Burgi Mamlukes as they were garrisoned at the Citadel (Burg means tower or fortress in Arabic).[29]

Sultan Barquq sought legitimacy in the eyes of the people by constantly associating himself with the former Bahri Mamluke rulers, especially Qalawun. In fact, he married Baghdad Khatun, a widow of the Sultan Sha'ban and one of the last remaining descendents of the Sultan Qalawun. He continued the Bahri military campaigns to fend off the Crusaders and the Mongols and further promoted Sunni Islam.

Barquq died in 1399 and was succeeded by his son Farag ibn Barquq who inherited the throne at a very young age. [30] Farag rule went down in history as one of the worst for Egypt as his reign was characterized by constant conflict. He was deposed and killed in Damascus, Syria at the age of twenty-three. Still, he did manage to move his father's body from his mosque on Bayn al Qasyryn Street near Khan al Khalili bazaar to his complex in the Northern Cemetery in accordance with his father's wishes.

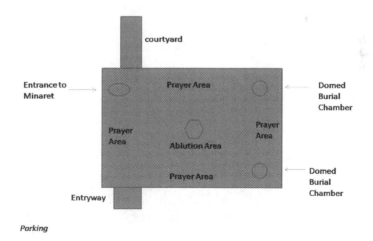

Layout of Sultan Barquq Complex

29 The Bahri Mamlukes were given their name because they were based on the island of Rhoda on the Nile. "Bahr" means sea, water or river in Arabic.

30 Some sources say that Farag was ten when he succeeded to throne while others claim that he was thirteen.

Description

The madrasa of Sultan Barquq's complex contained areas for each of the four rites of Islam to be taught. The twin minarets rise high above the structure, their first half in rectangular form and the top half circular. The two tombs contain the remains of Barquq and his sons, Farag and Abd al'Aziz, in one chamber, and the remains of two of Farag's daughters, Shiriz and Shakra, in the other. The twin chambers are lit by a group of stained glass windows framed with stucco. The fact that men and women are buried in separate chambers demonstrates that the sexes were kept apart even in death, a custom still in practice today.

Sultan Barquq Complex

The Barquq complex was also an attempt to urbanize an area that was largely desert at the time it was built. This allowed the complex to be designed without size restraints. Included in the design for the complex were not only living quarters, but baths, bakeries, markets, grain mills, and rooms for visitors, all of which were to be connected by a series of alleys and streets. The Sultan, however, did not live to see the completion of the full design of the complex. Still, the complex was enormous, covering some 5,329 square meters (17,719 square feet), making it the largest monument in the Northern Cemetery.

Before entering the monument, take time outside to appreciate the monumental size of the complex. At the entrance is a sign with a diagram of the building installed by the Egyptian Antiquities Organization during the structure's renovation. Once inside, turn down the long hallway on your left. As you enter the hall, notice the carved stone from a pharaonic monument used as a doorstep. The idea behind its use is to crush the pagan religion in a literal and figurative sense. Further on, the hall changes from being vaulted to having a flat wooden roof. Part of this roof has been restored, albeit poorly, with brown paint covering what was once a decorated surface.

After a lengthy hall, the complex opens up into a square sanctuary with each side measuring 240 feet. The structure is four stories high with cells for Sufis located off the courtyard. The open court is square in shape and is bordered on all sides by arcades and chambers. The arcades have both rounded and pointed arches. Under these arcades, the four rites of Islam were historically taught. In the middle of the courtyard, a water fountain is in bad need of repair. At the back of the courtyard is the sanctuary with pulpit, prayer niche and balcony. The prayer niche is marble surrounded by four columns (two on each side) and is covered by a small, ribbed dome. The lack of decoration on the components of the area of prayer is characteristics of Sufis who did not want any distractions from their devotion to God. A later addition, the pulpit is decorated with ivory inlay in an arabesque pattern. It was donated by the Sultan Qaytbay in 1483 and is unusual for the time in that the decoration is carved in stone rather than wood. The *dikka* or balcony is made of wood and is at the edge of the sanctuary.

The tomb-chambers occupy the back corners and are topped by two of the earliest and largest stone domes in Cairo. The chambers are separated from the sanctuary by beautiful mashrabiya screens carved in a six pointed star pattern. The southern mausoleum is for the women of the Barquq family and contains three cenotaphs for Barquq's two daughters and their nurse. The tall dome is decorated with calligraphy and other geometric patterns. These black and red painted patterns were made to look like inlaid marble which is commonly used to decorate other parts of Islamic buildings but would have been much too heavy for the dome to support. Poor restoration work takes away from the beauty of the dome.

The circular room is lighted by stained glass windows decorated with Islamic calligraphy in the center. Move your eyes across the room and see how the identical windows appear completely different depending on the amount of light they are receiving. Also, take time to look at the varying and intricate designs painted on the wooden beams that hold the light fixtures and also admire the marble floor tiles decorated with different geometric designs. The prayer niche is of striped marble in alternating red, black and white.

Barquq's mausoleum is very similar to the women's tomb chamber. It contains four cenotaphs that are in good condition. Barquq and his son Faraj are both buried here. Barquq's cenotaph has a tall phallic symbol that is covered with Islamic calligraphy which discusses Barquq's life and requests that God look favorably upon him. The dome is more colorful than its twin in the women's chamber and is decorated with a combination of geometric symbols and Islamic calligraphy.

Return to the courtyard and head to the north-west corner of the complex. Here, you will find a door that leads upstairs. Go up one flight and you will find a charming balcony. This is a nice place to sit for a few minutes and contemplate all that you have seen and to imagine the complex when it was an active religious community of Sufi monks. The wooden railings of the balcony are mostly original. From the balcony, there is a good view of the neighboring War Cemetery as well as the small, domed tomb of Sultan Barquq's father Anas, once connected to the main building by an arcade.

As you continue your ascent to the roof, stop at the second floor and climb across some of the ruins of the cells that once housed the Sufi monks. This part of the complex provides a good vantage point from which to inspect the carved zigzag pattern of the domes. This pattern replaced the use of ribs and represents a significant advancement in Mamluke building.

The stairs continue to the roof where visitors not only have an encompassing view of the entire Barquq complex, but a good vantage point from which to look over the surrounding semi-urbanized area of the City of the Dead. From here, it is apparent how more modern structures housing the living have crept between the older monuments.

Visitors can climb one of the two minarets for an even better vantage point. The second minaret was badly damaged in an earthquake in 1992.

Access to Visitors

Barquq's complex houses a popular, working mosque. It is best, therefore, for visitors to avoid prayer times when they will be refused entry. The Barquq complex has undergone significant restorations and was opened to the public with some fanfare by the Egyptian Antiquities Organization with the hope of making it a popular site for tourists. Unfortunately, visitors are still few and far between. There is, however, an appointed care-taker and visitors will be required to purchase a ticket upon entering (at the time of publication a ticket for foreigners was LE 3, students LE 1.50). Visitors can usually persuade the care-taker to allow them to go on the roof of the complex. A small tip will be expected for this service. Visitation hours are generally from 8 AM to 4 PM with the exception of prayer times, especially on Fridays.

THE COMPLEX OF SULTAN BARSBAY

Upon leaving Barquq's complex, turn left and walk a few hundred meters. On your left will be a dusty complex surrounded by wrought iron fencing. This is the Mosque and Mausoleum of the Sultan al-Ashraf Barsbay.

History

Al-Ashraf Abu Al-Nasr Barsbay was a Circassian who was originally bought by a Jewish merchant and brought to Aleppo in Syria. After being sold again, he ended up in Cairo with Barquq as his master and became a member of the royal garrison housed at the Citadel. During the reign of the Mamluke Sultan Al-Muyyad Shaykh he was given the title of Prince and then became the Vice-Sultan of Tripoli in 1418. Under the rule of Sultan Al-Salih Mohammad Ibn Tatr, he was appointed Dawadar and then Vice-Sultan of Egypt. He finally became Sultan in 1422 and ruled for an unusually long sixteen stable years.

Barsbay's reign is known for the defeat of European pirates based in Cyprus who had long disrupted Muslim shipping routes in the eastern Mediterranean. Barsbay also developed a flourishing trade with Persia and India, turning trade in certain spices into a state monopoly and bringing much wealth to Egypt. Barsbay also stopped the practice of the transfer of land between rulers and began minting his own currency known as *Al-Ashrafiyya*.

Barsbay's rule ended in 1438 and his mortuary complex was constructed in 1432 in the Northern Cemetery. It was made to accommodate only about seventeen Sufis. Its madrasa provided training for Sufi students who were studying the Hanafi rite of Sunni Islam.

Description

Like Barquq's, Barsbay's complex consists of a mausoleum, a madrasa, and two sabils. The madrasa-mosque is very elegant in appearance, containing two liwans (vaulted spaces) with a path down the center separated by a pair of arcades. The madrasa contained living quarters for the Sultan and his Sufi sheikh, with attached quarters for Sufi disciples. The architecture and interior decoration is very impressive. The complex is known for its marble mosaic pavements as well as for the height and ornamentation of the main dome of the mausoleum. The interlacing pattern carved on the outside of the dome is a star motif and was the first of its kind. It is also unique because of its unusual elongated shape.

Complex of Barsbay

Take time to admire this structure from the outside as you will not be able to access the roof for a close inspection of the dome and minaret. The dome is painstakingly carved with interlocking geometric shapes that form an undulating star pattern. This design is a shift from the dominant zigzag pattern of most domes of the period. Pay special attention to the lowest row of carvings on the dome as there is an unfinished rosette. Experts of Islamic art and architecture claim that this unfinished rosette is evidence that the carvings were done after the dome itself was constructed and not during the construction. The minaret was built later than the rest of the complex and is in the Ottoman style. To those familiar with the Islamic architecture of the period, it appears significantly out of place with the rest of the complex.

From the main street, pass through the wrought iron gate in front of the main portal and access the complex. From the reception, enter the mosque-madrasa. This room will immediately strike you as completely different from the other major Mamluke complexes of the Northern Cemetery. Unlike the open courtyards of Inal, Qurqumus and Barquq, Barsbay's mosque-madrasa is long and narrow. The center aisle sinks beneath the two rows of arched arcades that border it. The columns supporting these arches have classical capitals in Greco-Roman style.

On either side of the center aisle are two raised liwans. The simple prayer niche is to your right. The pulpit, a later addition to the mosque dating to 1953, is said to be one of the finest in Cairo with its beautiful inlay of ivory in a star motif. Take notice of the fine floor that is covered by rugs (feel free to lift up the rugs at the corners). It is made of black and white marble, red and orange limestone, blue faience and mother of pearl. Also, notice the carved stucco windows with stained glass. The ceiling of painted wood is probably the result of restoration work during the Ottoman period. The chamber is lit by two rows of windows. The upper row has been restored with modern stained glass.

At the end of the center aisle is the tomb chamber. Barsbay's light gray marble cenotaph sits in this circular room built in typical Mamluke style. The prayer niche, a combination of marble and mother of pearl, is more highly decorated than its counterpart in the mosque. The dome appears to rise into the sky and the room is illuminated by traditional windows of carved stucco with the later addition of stained glass.

To the south of the mosque and mausoleum are the remains of the rab' or apartment complex. These apartments were each two stories high and had a toilet. The upper floors have windows that look out over the main road.

Access to Visitors

At the time of publication, access to this complex is unregulated. Whereas the complex is sometimes open and non-Muslim visitors are allowed in, the entrance is frequently kept locked. If locked, questioning passersby about the whereabouts of the key may produce positive results.

THE COMPLEX OF SULTAN QAYTBAY

Leaving Barsbay's complex, turn left and follow the road as it curves among the tombs and shops of this urbanized area of the cemetery. Don't be surprised to see barbers cutting hair, coffee shops, shoe shops, and even jewelry stores nestled among or inside of the tombs. As the road widens into a square, the striped facade of the Mosque and Mausoleum of the Sultan Qaytbay will appear before you.

The complex of the Amir Qurqumas are similar in arrangement to this neighboring complex of the Sultan Qaytbay, but lack the ornamentation and genius for which Qaytbay's mausoleum is renowned.

History

The complex of the Sultan al-Ashraf Qaytbay is the most celebrated mausoleum of the Northern Cemetery. It is here where the height of Mamluke achievement in art and architecture can be viewed.

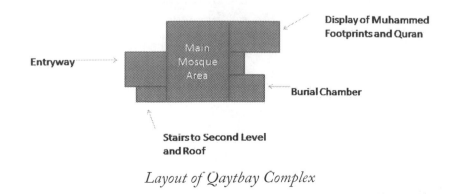

Layout of Qaytbay Complex

Qaytbay began his career as one of Barsbay's Mamlukes, bought for fifty dinars. Known for his combat skills, virility, and management abilities, he rose through the ranks of the Mamlukes to become Commander-in-Chief of the Army and ultimately, Sultan. Qaytbay reigned for 28 years which was longer than any other Mamluke sultan with the exception of Al-Nasir Muhammad (1299 – 1340). Qaytbay's reign was well known for the strong taxation of subjects that took place as some one third of Egypt's production was taken as tax, allowing Qaytbay to fund many building and restoration projects, Indeed, under his rule, the Muslim Empire witnessed a great period of building and restoration. Some 85 buildings are attributed to Qaytbay in Egypt and throughout the Middle East. During his reign as Sultan, Qaytbay developed relations with the Ottomans who were rising in power and controlled the spice trade between Europe and the Orient until the Portuguese discovered a sea route to India around Africa. During the last years of Qaytbay's rule, Cairo was hit hard by a great plague that took the lives of thousands of people, including his only wife and daughter. Distraught following the loss of his family, he died in 1496.

Qaytbay's complex in the Northern Cemetery dates from 1472-74 and once formed a large, enclosed compound consisting of nine buildings. Included in the original design were traveler's lodgings (that were rented to defray the cost of maintenance), a burial ground for members of the Sultan's family, drinking troughs for animals to be watered as well as waterwheels that supplied the complex. The tomb chamber contains fossilized footprints said to belong to the Prophet Muhammed. [31] In its early years the complex was surrounded by desert and was a popular stop on the trade routes between Egypt, the Red Sea, and Syria.

---

31   Some say that the footprints are actually from the Saqqara area of Egypt
     (currently outside of modern day Cairo) which was a burial ground of the
     Pharoahs.

Description

The main structure of Qaythay's complex (which appears on the Egyptian one pound note) consists of a mosque-madrasa, tomb chambers, and a courtyard. Attached to the mausoleum is a hall containing the tombs of the Sultan's four wives. The outside of the building is made of red and white striped masonry (ablaq), and on the inside, ornate decoration abounds. Floors, doors, walls, windows, and ceilings are flowered with geometric and arabesque designs, as well as with elegant Islamic calligraphy. The individual designs combine to form a stunning vision.

The Celebrated Qaytbay Complex

From the roof, the dome and minaret can be examined and the considerable size of the complex can be appreciated. The dome is considered to be the finest in all of Cairo. It has two intricately carved designs: a raised straight-lined star pattern [32] and a recessed lacework of floral arabesques. This ornate detail is painstakingly reproduced on the three-tiered, 130-foot high minaret. The minaret rises into the sky above the City of the Dead and provides a panoramic view of the Northern Cemetery.

Take time outside to appreciate how well all of the various parts of the complex combine to form a building that is perfectly proportioned. In particular, note the relation between the minaret and the dome, the charming striped masonry, and the large wooden door with its metal medallion.

Climb the stairs to the front entrance and reception area where you will be met by a care-taker and asked to remove your shoes. Take note of the restored wooden ceiling in the reception area. Make your way down the narrow hallway on your right and prepare yourself for the site that will greet you in the mosque-madrasa. The room is a splendid array of color. Take a moment and sit and enjoy the enormous beauty of this room. Decoration abounds – geometric designs, arabesques and Islamic calligraphy in various shades of golds, blues and reds cover virtually every inch of the surface of the walls and ceilings. Stained glass windows colored with pinks, yellows and greens illuminate the room.

The mosque-madrasa has a central court with two large liwans to the east and west and two smaller liwans to the north and south. The pulpit is crafted from stone but made to appear as if it is wooden. Its wooden doors are gracefully decorated with inlaid mother of pearl. The prayer niche is made of stone with ablaq inlaid patterns. There are two ornately carved and painted octagonal Islamic columns flanking the prayer niche. The pavement of the room is of white and black marble. Notice the beautifully carved wooden doorframes in this room.

---

32 The star pattern is used throughout the monument as a symbol of guidance for worshipers.

To the back of the mosque-madrasa is a door that leads to the tomb chambers. If it is locked, ask the care-taker to open it. Through the door to the left is Qaytbay's mausoleum. It boasts of two light gray cenotaphs (one surrounded by an impressive meshrabeya screen) and a large Qur'an stand made of wood with inlaid mother of pearl. There are also two footprints on display that are said to belong to the Prophet Muhammad. These "relics" of the Prophet are two blocks of basalt that are said to be from Mecca with one bearing a bare foot print and the other a shoe print. The room itself has marble pavements on the lower walls. The upper walls and dome are decorated with Islamic calligraphy and geometric designs. The prayer niche is paneled, carved and painted stone flanked by two octagonal Islamic columns made of light gray marble.

Upon leaving this room, head down the stairs to an open courtyard. Hidden behind a mashrabiya screen built into a wall is the mausoleum of the women of Qaytbay's family, including his two younger sisters. This tomb chamber has five cenotaphs, all in desperate need of repair.

Return to the main entrance and ask the care-taker to be allowed to go upstairs. You will be allowed to wear your shoes for this part of the tour as the stairway is dark and the stairs themselves are in need of repair. On the first floor there is a balcony – which once served as a kuttab – that looks over the neighboring community. From here you can watch residents of the City of the Dead smoking waterpipes in the neighboring coffee shop or watch young girls fetch water from the community water tap.

From the roof you can inspect the dome – considered to be the finest in all of Cairo. This dome is a unique combination of two intricately carved designs: a raised, straight-lined, six pointed star pattern; and a recessed lacework of floral arabesques. This detail is reproduced on the three-tiered, 130 foot (40 meters) high minaret. Visitors can climb the 54 steps to the minaret's second balcony and enjoy the view of Qaytbay's complex. Remnants of the enclosure walls of the complex as well as an apartment building and watering trough are all visible.

Access to Visitors

This mosque and mausoleum is under the supervision of the Egyptian Antiquties Organization. Similar to Barquq's complex, there is a care-taker and a formal entrance fee (LE 3 foreigners, LE 1.5 students). If you wish to take photographs, a special ticket must be purchased. The care-taker will allow you to climb to the roof so that you can examine the detail of the minaret (which you can also climb) as well as the dome. If locked, request that it be opened. The roof provides a stunning view of the Northern Cemetery in its entirety. The mausoleum may also be locked and the care-taker will open the door upon request. Once again, it is practical to avoid prayer times as this mosque is the most popular in the community.

THE TOMB OF PRINCESS TUGHAY

This shrine is more difficult to locate. Leaving Qaytbay's complex turn and walk south so that Qaytbay is to your right. The road will narrow but continue until you find a large street. Turn right. Walk straight and take your second left. Then, take your second right. Soon, you will find a large, vaulted, liwan flanked by two domes. This is the Tomb of the Princess Tughay.

History

Princess Tughay is also known as Om Anuk (the mother of Anuk). She was the beloved wife of the Mamluke Sultan Al-Nasir Muhammed. Tughay was a Mongol who Sultan Al-Nasir married in order to cement a peace treaty with Iran. She soon became his favorite wife. Author/Historian William Lyster writes the following about Princess Tughay:

"She was renowned for her great beauty, as well as for her piety, and was able to capture the attention of the sultan, becoming in time his favorite wife. After the death of her husband, Tughay devoted her life to performing charitable acts, the most enduring being the foundation of the khanqah that surrounds her tomb. This impressive structure was completed in 1348, the same year that the Princess Tughay died of bubonic plague."[33]

At one time, Princess Tughay's complex was a large compound complete with a Sufi monastery. Today, all that survives is a liwan and the domed tomb chamber.

The Remains of the Complex of Princess Tughay

---

33   Lyster, William, "The City of the Dead", Cairo Today, March 1998, page 28.

Description

Not much is left of the major complex that once existed. Still, by focusing on the remaining parts, one can imagine what the larger complex must have looked like. Picture a large courtyard with a prominent entryway and minaret. Imagine a liwan and domed tomb chamber opposite those that still exist. This was the complex of Princess Tughay.

There are numerous architectural and stylistic components of this tomb to notice. The style of the dome over the burial chamber represents the most popular style of Mamluke dome in the 14th century. It is made of brick with external ribbing and is wide and high. This type of dome pre-dated the stone domes of the other major complexes of the Northern Cemetery. Also, notice the remnants of the colorful mosaic tile inscription inlaid in the ribbing of the dome. This type of decoration was more common in Iran and is evidence of Tughay's Mongolian ancestry. More evidence of Iranian influence is found in the stucco work with the design of peony flowers that covers the remaining liwan.

Access to Visitors

The tomb is surrounded by a wooden picket fence and is best admired from the outside. As stated earlier, it is in poor condition but is one of the original and most important monuments of the Northern Cemetery. It is under the supervision of the Egyptian Antiquities Organization but there is no permanent care-taker and no formal visiting hours or entrance fee.

CHAPTER 6

Markets, Moulids and Everyday Life

- *The Bird Market*
- *The Antiques ("Junk") Market*
- *The Moulids of Sayyida Nafisa, the*
- *Imam Al-Shafi'I*
- *and Sayyida Ruqayya*

EVERYDAY LIFE IN THE CITY OF THE DEAD

There are numerous events that happen in the City of the Dead in modern times that visitors can attend for additional cultural and religious experiences. These events demonstrate the continued importance of the City of the Dead in the lives of Cairenes as well as the functions of the City of the Dead beyond its use as cemeteries.

On Thursdays and Fridays, it is fascinating to observe the various entrances to the cemeteries as hordes of women dressed in black galabiyyas (long, traditional robes) as well as children come to the cemeteries to visit the dead of their families. People will sell assorted greens at the cemeteries' gates for the visitors/mourners to buy and place on the family tombs. In addition, these women can frequently be seen burning incense at the tombs or cooking food and celebrating a meal among the graves of their ancestors.

When visiting the various monuments of the City of the Dead, it is interesting to take time out to experience the modern life of the cemeteries as well. Visitors can have a glass of tea and smoke the waterpipe at numerous coffee shops throughout the cemeteries (two favorites are across the street from Sultan Qaytbay Mosque and Mausoleum and next to Sayyida Nafisa Mosque and Mausoleum); can shop in the shoe store or enjoy a *tamia* (deep-fried vegetable puree) sandwich along the main road between Sultan Barsbay and Sultan Qaytbay in the Northern Cemetery, and; can enjoy shopping at fruit and vegetable stalls at the northern tip of the Southern Cemetery near Sayyida Aisha Square.

For anyone who spends any significant time in the City of the Dead, you are sure to meet some of its residents and may be invited to share a cup of tea and a snack. Take advantage of the opportunity to enter into the lives of the residents of these cemetery communities. As stated in the introductory chapter of this book, these people of the City of the Dead will likely be as interested in you as you are of them and expect nothing in return for their hospitality.

Visitors can also bring home souvenirs from the City of the Dead. Two of the best places for such souvenirs are the blown glass factory to the right hand side of the main entrance to Qaytbay's mosque and mausoleum in the Northern Cemetery and numerous pottery shops in the Southern and Basateen Cemeteries. At the blown glass factory, there is a small shop that sells various types of deep blue colored dishes, vases and other creations made of blown glass. These items can be bought at inexpensive prices and the shop's proprietors speak some English. Custom design orders are taken. When visiting the shop, be sure to ask to see the actual workshop next door where visitors can witness the glass being blown into shape over hot flames. In the Southern and Basateen Cemeteries, there are numerous places where traditional pottery is sold. Popular with tourists are the various types of vases with hand-painted flowers and other designs gracing the surfaces. These are also relatively inexpensive but buyers should be prepared to barter for their purchases.

THE BIRD AND JUNK MARKETS

Each week, there are two popular markets that take place in the City of the Dead, both in the Southern Cemetery.

On Thursday mornings, there is a market that is popularly known as the "Bird Market". This *souk* takes place at the north-west tip of the Southern Cemetery (near the Citadel) on the main road venturing into the Cemetery from Sayyida Aisha Square. This market, also known as the Sayyida Aisha animal market, has booths and vendors with various kinds of birds, seed and other pets for sale as well as items similar to those for sale at "dollar shops" in the West. It is fascinating to walk through this market and see all of the various types of birds and animals for sale as well as the Egyptians who are simply out for a stroll through the market or who are engaging in a lengthy bartering process in search of a bargain. Whereas the Bird Market is a good place to witness traditional Egyptian commerce in action, it is also the site of a less reputable trade. Unfortunately, the Bird Market has come to represent the main outlet for illegal trade in animals. Many endangered species of birds, reptiles and mammals have been found for sale at the Sayyida Aisha market and often under horrifying conditions. A visit by the Tortoise Trust, an organization dedicated to the conservation of endangered tortoises, found Egyptian tortoises commonly on sale at the market in the Southern Cemetery. Egyptian tortoises are the most endangered species of tortoises in the Mediterranean region and are banned from commercial trade. Still, on one visit by the Tortoise Trade, they documented "approximately 300 Testudo kleinmanni (Egyptian tortoises) on open sale at prices between 5 and 10 Egyptian pounds each (less than 3 USD)".[34]

On Friday mornings, the Southern Cemetery is also home to the popular Antique or "Junk" Market. In Arabic, the market is popularly referred to as "*Souk al-Harameya*", or the "Thieve's Market". Here, visitors can mingle with Egyptians looking for a bargain on new, second-hand and sometimes even stolen items. Photographer Ed Kashi describes the market accordingly, "The Friday market is a scrap heap of modern detritus where it's possible to construct an entire automobile from scratch or develop a hybrid hairdryer that could double as a vacuum cleaner. It seems fitting in this graveyard of recycled tombs that the weekly market is

---

34 Tortoise Trade, Report on Inspection Visit to Sayyida Aisha Market, Cairo, June 1997.

a cluttered heap of odds and ends, bits and scraps, broken shards waiting to be reborn in some new context."[35]

Journalist Fayza Hassan paints a similar picture when describing the market. She notes;

> "Anything at all that has found its way into a garbage can, having admittedly outlived its usefulness, reappears here vested with a brand new mission. Old instant coffee jars are sold in bulk for glass recycling or by the piece for pickling and jam making, old bottles become candle holders, an old topless garden table inspires the do-it-yourself home decorator, an empty perfume bottle is raised to the rank of collector's item. Even old shoes are resoled, painted, varnished and occupy their rightful place as perfectly serviceable, in a display, together with miscellaneous objects ranging from obsolete Coca Cola and beer bottles to back issues of popular magazines and instruction manuals on how to use your first computer."[36]

The market may seem disorganized and chaotic (which can be part of its charm) but there is actually an internal system of the vendors that regulates who displays what and where. In addition, vendors must pay a fee to display their items with the amount of the fee depending on the type of wares and the amount of space that they occupy. Whereas the market is a cultural attraction for tourists, it provides a valuable service to low income families of Cairo who can purchase basic goods and second-hand clothing and shoes at cheap prices. In addition, it provides a supplemental income for many of the vendors who work in this "informal economy".[37] The informal sector is large and plays

---

35 Quote taken from the website for Ed Kashi's photographs of the City of the Dead at http://www.atlasmagazine.com/photo/kashi_cairo

36 Hassan, Fayza, "Off the Beaten Track", Al-Ahram Weekly, 5 – 11 October 1995, page 12.

37 The informal economy is based on a description of the location within which actors operate. Four categories of actors are typically identified:
- Home based workers
- Dependent home-base workers have the following characteristics:

an important role in Egypt, providing some 40% of Egypt's non-agricultural sector jobs. [38] Indeed, many of the vendors in the market have finished high school or have university educations. Unable to find formal jobs in their fields, they have resorted to trade in the informal economy in order to survive. The vendors of this market are called "roba bechia" in Egyptian Arabic. Some of the older vendors have managed to do quite well with their informal sales and now boast of "formal" antique shops in other areas of Cairo.

This market was originally located in the same area as the Bird Market but was forced to move a few years ago. At present, it is located adjacent to and in the Southern Cemetery near the Mosque and Mausoleum of the Imam al-Shafi'i. The main part of the market is held under an overpass of the Austrade Highway as you head south from the Citadel. The area is known as *Al-Tunsi.* Following the move to this location, there was an attempt by the Government to formalize the market by having a private contractor take over the management of the market. This attempt failed, however. Apparently, no contractor was willing to pay the price of monthly rent that the Government requested. More recently, the Cairo governorate is seeking to move the market entirely, claiming that it is a refuge for criminals. In 2001, there was a proposal to move the market to Al-Qatamiya, some 60 kilometers from the center of Cairo. A more recent proposal is to move the market to

---

- they work at home outside the establishment that buys their products;
- they agree by prior arrangement to supply goods or services to a particular enterprise;
- their remuneration consists of the prices paid for their products
- they do not employ workers on a regular basis.
- Independent home-based workers are those who work in their   home and deliver their products or services to any prospective buyer. Their characteristics are those of the self-employed and are classified as part of the group "own-account workers".
- Street traders and street vendors
- Itinerant or seasonal or temporary job workers on building sites or road works
- Those in between the streets and home, e.g., waste collectors

38 This figure was taken from Business Monthly, the journal of the American Chamber of Commerce in Egypt where they cited a 1992 study by economist Heba Handoussa.

four separate locations outside of and on the fringes of Cairo. Both proposals have been met with opposition by both vendors and buyers alike of this Cairo tradition which brings Cairenes flocking to the City of the Dead every week.

Both markets start early in the morning (around 7 AM) and run into the afternoon.

MOULIDS

A *moulid* is a celebration of a holy person and literally means "birth" in Arabic. Moulids are celebrated by both Muslims and Coptic Christians in Egypt to honor their respective saints and typically take place on the anniversary of a saint's birth or, in some cases, on the anniversary of their death. Islamic moulids occur in accordance with dates on the Lunar Islamic calendar. Since 1976, the Supreme Council of Sufis Orders has been responsible for specifying the dates of moulids. Therefore, visitors who wish to attend a moulid should check local Egyptian newspapers for dates.

It is important to point out that many Muslims do not consider the celebration of moulids to be a proper religious custom. Rather, moulid festivals are more of a popular Egyptian tradition rather than an Islamic one. Islamic moulids were first celebrated by the Fatimid rulers (969-1171) who hosted a moulid to honor the Prophet Muhammad. Still, the moulid celebrations may have drawn on the tradition of pharaonic Egypt where annual celebrations for the Gods were held. Also, a moulid can be compared to the Christian celebration of Christmas. The Fatimid moulids were very formal and took place at the court of the government. Today, moulids are concentrated around the tombs of saints, have more of a festival atmosphere and all are invited to attend. The most significant moulids are *Moulid al-Nabi* which commemorates the Prophet Muhammad's birthday and the Moulid al-Husein which honors the Prophet's grandson Husein.

The celebration of moulids combines an interesting combination of food, games, music and dance and religious contemplation. Egyptians celebrating a moulid typically eat special moulid sweets called *Halawet al-Moulid* and *hummus* (ground chick peas) and there are special candy dolls called *Aroussa al Moulid* (Bride of the Moulid) for children. There are typically rides such as ferris wheels, pellet-gun shooting galleries and swings as well as other entertainment activities set up for the enjoyment of children and adults. Other more serious customs, such as that of circumcision, have also been associated with moulids.

The Sufis tend to play a role large in the celebration of moulids with public processions, parades of Sufi Orders, *hadras* (Sufi rituals), *zikr* (ritual dance) and *Inshad* and *Dhikir* (Sufi chanting). Sufi rituals take place in various colorful *sowans* or tents. One common ritual consists of Sufis swaying their bodies back and forth to the beat of drums and tambourines as Sufi *Munshideen* (singers) chant. The following is an account of this Sufi ritual:

> At nightfall, after the evening prayer, the followers gather in the tents of the brotherhoods to practice the Dhikr: barefoot, with their shoes disposed in the middle of the mat, the disciples place themselves side-by-side; prayers and praises are pronounced, the names of Allah are repeated in unison, at the rhythm of a chant of love directed by a sufi singer. The remembrance of God, by the repetition of His names purifies the soul and prepares it to receive the divine presence. A song of absolute love for Allah rises from each assembly. Back and forth, in and out, the disciples move their bodies at an increasing speed as the tempo of drums and tambourines quickens. They experience various psychological states: pain, joy, effacement, bliss; the inner pilgrimage culminates in an ecstasy of fusion with Allah. And the state of trance occurs..."[39]

The Sufi inclusion of music and song during worship at moulids is controversial and considered inappropriate by some. Still, the masses in Egypt believe that moulids are an acceptable form of religious

---

39 This was taken from "The Great Jihad: Sufism and popular islam in Egypt"on the website http://nnilsson free.fr/mouled3/index2.html. No author is noted but the description adequately describes what the other of this book has witnessed during moulids.

expression. Demonstrating the two minds of the practice, a historian described moulids as thus,

> "[Egyptians] set up masses of tents, booths, kitchens and coffee houses. There assembles a huge world of the middle class, the elite, the lower orders of the city, peasants, and peddlers of diversion, games, dancing-girls and whores, monkey-masters and snake-charmers. They fill the empty areas and the gardens, defile the tombs, urinate and defecate, committing adultery and buggery. They dance to drums and whistles day and night. Jurists and scholars join in and are imitated by the highest of princes, the most prominent merchants, and the general public with demur. Indeed they believe that [all this] is a mean to proximity (*qurba*) to God and a form of worship. Were it not for this fact, the ulama [Muslim scholars trained in Islamic laq] would not have kept silent, and certainly would not have taken part. May God guide us all."[40]

The pinnacle of a moulid is the *Leila el-Kebira* or Big Night. This is the last day of the celebration and when the most Sufi performances occur.

In Egypt, there is an entire group of people whose lives revolve around the celebration of moulids. These people are called the *Mawalidiya* and they travel from one moulid to another setting up and dismantling the infrastructure for the celebrations. The mawalidiya include merchants, vendors and performers.

The moulid season in Egypt lasts for approximately five months each year.

Some of the moulids in Egypt take place in the Muslim cemeteries of the City of the Dead. The most important of those are in celebration of Sayyida Nafisa and the Imam al-Shafi'i. These moulids

---

40 This quote was taken from "For the Love of God" by Fayza Hassan in Al-Ahram Weekly On-line, 21-27 December 2000. The quote is attributed to the historian El-Gabarti and was recorded in the book <u>Sufism and Islamic Reform in Egypt</u> by Julian Johansen, Oxford 1996.

typically attract many sick people as well as others seeking spiritual intervention and baraka. There is also an annual moulid that is less well attended at the tomb of Sayyida Ruqayya.

Although not a religious figure, the atmosphere at the tomb of Abdel Halim al-Hafez is quite similar to a moulid on the occasion of the anniversary of his death (March 30th). At this time, members of his family are typically present at the tomb and much music and singing takes place.

ABOUT THE AUTHOR

Jeffrey A. Nedoroscik grew up in Sutton, Massachusetts. He attended the College of the Holy Cross in Worcester, Massachusetts majoring in Political Science with concentrations in Middle Eastern Studies and Peace & Conflict Studies. He graduated in 1992. During his junior year, he was the first Holy Cross student to study abroad at the American University in Cairo for one semester. During that time, he befriended people living in the Southern Cemetery of the City of the Dead.

Upon graduation from Holy Cross, Mr. Nedoroscik was awarded a Thomas J. Watson fellowship. This fellowship allowed him to return to Cairo and to look more closely at the lives of the people living in the informal communities of the City of the Dead. His research led to the publication of the book *The City of the Dead: A History of Cairo's Cemetery Communities* (Bergin & Garvey, Westport, CT. 1997).

In 1994, Mr. Nedoroscik began working with the United States Agency for International Development (USAID) in Cairo, the economic aid arm of the U.S. State Department. At the same time, he continued researching and writing and also attended graduate classes at the American University in Cairo. In 1996, Mr. Nedoroscik was awarded a Sasakowa Peace Foundation fellowship. The fellowship provided funding for Mr. Nedoroscik to conduct a comparison of the Islamic fundamentalist movement in Upper Egypt and the Zapatista rebellion in Chiapas, Mexico. The report of this study, *Lessons in Violent Internal Conflict: Egypt and Mexico*, was chosen as one of the best fellowship reports and published in Japan.

Mr. Nedoroscik accepted a position with USAID's Mission in Kigali, Rwanda in 1998 and worked there for nearly three years which included short term assignments that took him throughout sub-Saharan Africa.

In 2000, Mr. Nedoroscik was named the Supervisory Executive Officer for the USAID Mission in Zagreb, Croatia, where he would work for seven years.

Following September 11th, Mr. Nedoroscik wrote an article entitled "Extremist Groups in Egypt" that looks at the roots of Islamic terrorism, using the Egyptian experience as an example, and which provides insight into how terrorism can be combated. This article first appeared in the Frank Cass Journal *Terrorism and Political Violence* (London, 2003) and was reprinted in the United States in *Annual Editions: Violence and Terrorism 04/05* (McGraw Hill, 2004).

In 2008, Mr. Nedoroscik moved to Washington DC and accepted a position as the Special Assistant to USAID's Chief Acquisition Officer and Procurement Executive for a period of one year. During that year, he worked on many high level activities and also traveled to Jordan and Iraq. Mr. Nedoroscik was then asked to travel to Sudan and conduct a management assessment of the operations there. This temporary duty assignment turned into a 5+ month stint as the Acting Management Officer at the US Consulate in Juba. Upon return to the USA, Mr. Nedoroscik began working for USAID's Office of Overseas Management Staff. In this capacity, he continued to support Sudan, as well as the Afghanistan-Pakistan Task Force, worked on the Joint Management Council with the Department of State as well as on Secretary Clinton's Quadrennial Diplomacy and Development Review. Continuing to assist overseas missions, Mr. Nedoroscik traveled to Yemen to be the Acting Executive Officer at the USAID mission. He later was part of a Pacific Island Assessment Team which traveled to Fiji, Samoa, Australia, New Zealand and Papua New Guinea to make recommendations for the location of a new USAID regional mission to the Pacific Islands.

Mr. Nedoroscik has been the recipient of numerous awards including five Meritorious Honor Awards, a Superior Honor Award and two Special Act Awards from the US Government.

Jeffrey A. Nedoroscik is an employee of the United States Government. All opinions and views expressed herein are those of the Author and not necessarily those of the United States Agency for International Development or any other U.S. Government agency.

GLOSSARY OF TERMS

Ablaq	wall striped masonry in two alternating colors, usually black and white and red and ochre
Abbasid	The Abbasid Dynasty ruled the Arab world between A.D. 758 – 1288
Ablution	Washing before prayer 5 times a day in accordance with Islamic rites. Also, the washing of the body prior to burial.
Al-Fustat	the capital city of Egypt prior to the founding of al-Qahira or Cairo
al-Qahira	literally meaning "the Victorious", al-Qahira was the name given to the city founded by the Fatimids in A.D. 969 that would later become known around the world as Cairo
Amir	Arabic word for prince. A high ranking military commander.
Amir Kabir	Commander-in-Chief of the armies
Amir Tablkhana	"Amir of Forty" in Arabic; a military position
Aqueduct	a conduit that resembles a bridge but is made to carry water
Arabesque	ornamental design based on vegetal forms in which leaves and stems form a reciprocal, continuous interlacing pattern

Ayyubids	a ruling Dynasty in Egypt between A.D. 1171 – 1250 named after the founder, Salah al-Din al-Ayyubi (Saladin)
Bab	door in Arabic
Backsheesh	tips (see footnote 11 for further explanation)
Bahri Mamlukes	A succession of strong Mamluke sultans who controlled Egypt and Syria between A.D. 1250 – 1382. The reign of the Bahri Mamlukes was characterized by stability and prosperity as well as a powerful military.
Baraka	blessing or good luck usually associated with a holy person or holy site
Bilharzia	an infestation caused by a parasite with a resulting infection
Burgi Mamlukes	The Burgi Mamlukes took over from the Bahri Mamlukes in A.D. (Circassian) 1382 and rules Egypt until 1517. The reign of the Burgi Mamlukes was characterized by epidemic outbreaks and high taxation.
Caliph	successor to the Prophet
Cenotaph	a symbolic tomb
Circassian	a member of a Caucasian people living in the Caucasus but not speaking an Indo-European language
Citadel	a fortress
Coptic	The modern use of the term "Coptic" refers to both Egyptian Christians themselves, and the final stage of the language of the Ancient Egyptians.
Cruciform Plan	a typical plan for a mosque that consists of four vaulted liwans that face each other across a central courtyard
Crusaders	warriors who engage in holy war, used here to refer to the European holy wars of the

	High Middle Ages that sought to conquer other lands and spread Christianity.
Dawadar	An Amir from among the men who share in the group feeling of the ruler. The ruler usually relies upon on him, trusts him, and confides in him.
Dhikir	Sufi chanting
Dikka	ritual platform where the ritual postures of the imam and responses are repeated so that the larger congregation can follow
Fatimids	a Shi'ite Dynasty that originated in North Africa and ruled Egypt from A.D. 969 to 1171
Hadras	Sufi rituals
Hippodrome	a stadium used for sports events such as horse races
Howsh	a courtyard
Imam	the man who leads prayer at a mosque
Inshad	Sufi chanting; melodic vocalization
Khanqah	residential institution especially endowed for Sufis
Kufic	the earliest form of Islamic calligraphy
Kursi	a stand that a Qur'an is displayed on
Kuttab	Qur'anic school
Lelia el-Kabira	"Big Night" in Arabic; the last night of a moulid celebration
Liwan	a vaulted hall closed on three sides and open on one side overlooking the courtyard of a mosque
Madrasa	A religious school endowed for teaching all four sects of Islamic interpretation. These four schools are Shafi'ie, Maliki, Hanafi and Wahabi.

Mamluke	Literally means "owned by another". Mamlukes were slaves imported from Asia, trained, freed and recruited into the military service.
Mashrabiya	Originally a place for drinking, mashrabiya is commonly used to designate the turned or carved wooden latticed work window screens typically in traditional Islamic domestic architecture. The window screens provided privacy to women inside the homes from passers-by.
Mausoleum	a large stately tomb or a building housing such a tomb or several tombs
Mawalidiya	people who travel from one moulid to another setting up and dismantling the infrastructure for the festivals
Mecca	holy Islamic city in Saudi Arabia
Meuzziun	Islamic religious authority who conducts marriages
Mihrab	an arched niche or recess in the qibla wall of a mosque indicating the direction of Mecca
Minaret	the tower of a mosque from which the call to prayer was traditionally made from five times a day in accordance with Islamic rites
Minbar	the pulpit in a mosque from which the sermon at the Friday prayers is given
Monastery	a community of persons, especially monks, bound by vows to a religious life and often living in partial or complete seclusion; the dwelling place of such a community.
Mosque	a Muslim house of worship
Moulid	religious fair in celebration of a saint's birthday
Munshideen	Sufi singers who perform at moulids

Nubia	an ancient region of northeastern Africa along the Nile River made up of southern Egypt and northern Sudan.
Oboe	a slender woodwind instrument with a conical bore and a double-reed mouthpiece, having a range of three octaves and a penetrating, poignant sound
Ottomans	Western Asian tribes of Turkomen who established a powerful empire based in present day Turkey in the 15th century. The Ottomans rules Egypt from A.D. 1517 to 1800.
Portal	doorway
Qasr	"palace" in Arabic
Qibla	the direction of prayer oriented towards Mecca, Saudi Arabia
Qibla Wall	the wall in a mosque facing the direction of Mecca, Saudi Arabia as indicated by the mihrab
Qur'an	the Muslim holy book
Quraysh	the clan of the Prophet Muhammad
Rab'	apartment building or tenement
Ramadan	the Muslim holy month that commemorates the revelation of the Qur'an to the Prophet Muhammad
Sabil	a small building consisting of a public water dispensary
Sabil-Kuttab	A structure combining a water dispensary on the ground floor and a school above it. This type of structure was first introduced in Cairo in Mamluke times as an attached part of mosques and were made free standing during the Ottoman period.

Shi'ite	Muslims who believe that Ali was the rightful successor to the Prophet Muhammad
Souk	"market" in Arabic
Sowan	colorful tents where Sufi rituals are held during moulids
Stalactite	An ornamental arrangement of multi-tiered niches found on domes, squinches and portals
Stucco	carved plaster used as low-relief decoration on ceiling or walls
Sufi	Muslim ascetics bound to lead a communal life of prayer and poverty
Sultan	the highest ranking ruler of a Muslim state
Sunni	the branch of Islam that accepts the first four caliphs as rightful successors of the Prophet Muhammad
Zawiya	a residence for Muslim Sufis centered around a sheikh
Zikr	the ritual dance of Sufis
Ziyyarah	visitation of a holy shrine

USEFUL ARABIC PHRASES & WORDS

Fen al Bowab?	Where is the doorman?
Mumkin aruh fo?	Can I go upstairs?
Mumkin aruh gowwa?	Can I go inside?
Fen al gamma Barquq?	Where is the mosque of Barquq?
Mumkin sura?	Can I take a picture?
Ana ba-dawwar…	I am looking for…
Al moulid empta?	When is the moulid?
Bikan al tescara?	How much is the ticket?
Ilhaq ni!	Help me!
Mumkin fakka?	Can I have change?
Il bab maftuah?	Is the door open?
Fen Sharia _____?	Where is _____ Street?
Sabah il-xer	Good Morning
Izzayak?	How are you?
Ahlan	Greetings
Masalama	Goodbye
Ahlan Washalan	Glad to meet you
Ana Amrikani	I am American
Bardon	Pardon me
Hena	Here
Henak	There
Foe	Up
That	Down

Warra	Behind
Gamba	Near
Al-yameen	To the right
A-shimmel	To the left
Gowwa	Inside
Barra	Outside
Kwayyis	Good
Yalla	Let's Go (Come on)
Sawwa Taxi	Taxi Driver
Minfadlak	Please
Geneh	Egyptian Pound
Gamaa	Mosque
Arafa	Cemetery

NUMBERS

0	Sifr
1	Wahcd
2	Etnen
3	Talata
4	Arbaa
5	Xamsa
6	Sitta
7	Sabaa
8	Tamanya
9	Tesa
10	Ashara
20	Ashreen
30	Talateen
40	Arbayeen
50	Xamseen
60	Sitteen
70	Sabyeen
80	Tamaneen
90	Tayesieen
100	Miya

SELECTED BIBLIOGRAPHY

Abaza, Ismai. "The Complex of Sultan al-Ashraf Barsbay (Barsbey) In the Northern   Cemetery", Tour Egypt Feature on http://touregypt.net/featurestories/barsbayfuneral

Abaza, Ismail. "The Funerary Complex of Amir Qurqumus", Tour Egypt Feature on http://touregypt/featurestories/qurqumas.

Abaza, Ismail. "The Funerary Complex of Sultan al-Ashraf Qaytbay (Qaitbay) In the Northern Cemetery", Tour Egypt Feature on http://touregypt.net/featurestories/qaytbayfunerary.

Abaza, Ismail. "The Khanqah and Mausoleum of Sultan Faraj Ibn Barquq", Tour Egypt Feature on http://touregypt.net/featurestories/khanqahbarquq.

Abaza, Ismail. "Madrasa Khanqah of Sultan al-Zahir Barquq", Tour Egypt Feature on http://www.touregypt.net/featurestories/barquq.

Abaza, Ismail. "The Mausoleum of Imam al-Shafi'i", Tour Egypt Feature on http://www.touregypt.net/featurestories/shafii.

Abaza, Ismail. "Mosque/Madrasa, Sabil-Kuttab and Mausoleum Complex of Ashraf Barsbay", Tour Egypt Feature on http://www.touregypt.net/featurestories/barsbay.

Abaza, Ismail. "The Religious and Funerary Complex of Sultan al-Ashraf Inal in Cairo's Northern Cemetery, Tour Egypt Feature on http://touregypt.net/featurestories/inal.

"Abbasid Caliphs Mausoleum", ArchNet on http://www.archnet.org/library/sites.

Abu-Lughod, Janet, Cairo: 1001 Years of the City Victorious, Princeton, NJ: Princeton University Press, 1971.

Asmar, Samir, "Remembering Farid al-Atrash: A Contender in the Age of Giants", Al Jadid, Vol. 4, No. 22, 1988.

"The Art of the Fatimid Period (909-1171 A.D.)", Metropolitan Museum on http://www.metmuseum.org.

"The Art of the Mamluk Period (1250-1517 A.D.)", Metropolitan Museum on http://www.metmuseum.org.

Ash-Sha'rawi, Imam Metawalli. "Nafisa at-Tahira: Rare Lady Saint of the Egyptians" on http://www.sunnah.org/history/Scholars/nafisa_at_tahira.

Behrens-Abouseif, Dr. Doris. "The Family Mauseoleum of Muhammad 'Ali (Hawsh Al-Basha)" on http://www.akmb.gov.tr/turkce/books/osmanli/d.behrens.

Bizzari, Heba Fatteen. "Cities of the Dead", Tour Egypt Feature on http://www.touregypt.net/featurestories/city.

Cross, Dr. John C. "Egypt's neglected Engine in Growth", Business Monthly, Journal of the American Chamber of Commerce on http://www.openair.org/cross/egyptinf.

Danielson, Virginia Louise. "Umm Kulthum: An Outline of her Life", Ph.D. Thesis, University of Illinois, 1991, pages 57-75 on http://almashriq.hiof.no/egypt/700/780/umKoulthoum/biography.

Duncan, David J. "Scholarly Views on Sharjarat al-Durr" on http://www.library.cornell.edu/colldev/mideast/duncan.

El-Rashidi, Yasmine. "Market on the Move" Al-Ahram Weekly, Cairo, 2004, No. 691.

Ghazaleh, Pascale. "Digging for Paradise", Al-Ahram Weekly On-Line, 19-25 October 2000, Issue No. 504.

"The Great Jihad: Sufism and popular islam in Egypt" on http://nnilsson.free.fr/moulid.

Hassan, Fayza. "For the Love of God", Al-Ahram Weekly On-line, 21-27 December 2000, Issue No. 513.

Hassan, Fayza, "Off the Beaten Track", Al-Ahram Weekly, 5 – 11 October 1995, page 12.

Hoffman, Valerie J., "Saints and Sheikhs in Modern Egypt", Regional Issues Egypt at http://www.isim.nl/newsletter/2/regional/11.html.

"Hosh al-Pasha", ArchNet on
http://archnet.org/library/sites.

"Imam al-Shafi'I Mausoleum", ArchNet on
http://www.archnet.org/library/sites.

Iskander, Lara. "El Moulid", Tour Egypt Feature Story on
http://touregypt.net/featurestories/moulid.

Kashi, Ed. "City of the Dead" on
http://www.atlasmagazine.com/photo/kashi_cairo/kashi.

Lyseter, William, "The City of the Dead", Cairo
Today, March 1988, page 27.

Marsot, Afaf Lutfi Al-Sayyid. A Short History of Modern
Egypt, New York, NY: Cambridge University Press, 1985.

"Mausoleum of Imam Al-Shafi'I Home Guide: Rough guides
for entertainment, hotels, bars, restaurants, tourist attractions
and sites", on http://www.alpharooms.com/guide.

"Muhammad Ali", Encyclopedia of the Orient, Lexicorient.com.

Nedoroscik, Jeffrey. The City of the Dead: A
History of Cairo's Cemetery Communities,
Westport, CT: Bergin & Garvey, 1997.

Rashed, Dena. "Into Exile", Al-Ahram Weekly On-
Line, 8-14 March 2001, Issue No. 524.

Roussan, Rasheed. "On the 23rd Anniversary of Abdel
Halim Hafez's death", RomanySaad.com.

"Sayyida 'Atika and Muhammad al-Ja'fari Mashhad", ArchNet on
http://www.archnet.org/library/sites.

"Sayyida Ruqayya Mashad", ArchNet on
http://archnet.org/library/sites.

"Southern Cemetery (Al-Qarafrah al-Kubra)" on
http://www.caribbean-voyager.com/roughguide.

"Sultan Al-Ashraf Abu Al-Nasr Barsbay", Eternal Egypt on
http://www.eternalegypt.org/EternalEgyptWebsiteHome.

"Sultan al-Ashraf Inal Complex", ArchNet on
http://archnet.org/library/sites.

"Sultan Faraj ibn Barquq Funerary Complex", ArchNet on http://archnet.org/library/sites.

"Sultan Qansuh Abu Sa'id Mausoleum", ArchNet on http://archnet.org/library/sites.

"Surpassing Dreams", EGYPTmyway on http://www.egyptmyway.com/articles/cityofdead2.

Tortoise Trust. "Report on Inspection Visit to Saiyyida Aisha Market, Cairo, June 1997", on http://www.tortoisetrust.org/activities/cairo.

Weit, Gaston (translation by Seymour Feiler). Cairo: City of Art and Commerce, Norman, Oklahoma: University of Oklahoma Press, 1964.

Williams, Caroline. Islamic Monuments in Cairo: A Practical Guide, Fourth Edition, Cairo, Egypt: The American University in Cairo Press, 1983.